KINGS OF THE
IRON ROAD

KINGS OF THE IRON ROAD

Steam Passenger Trains of New Zealand

J.D. Mahoney

Edited by Philip Whyte

 *The Dunmore Press*

© J.D. Mahoney

First published in 1982
by
The Dunmore Press Limited
PO Box 5115
Palmerston North
New Zealand

Reprinted 1983
Reprinted 1987
Reprinted 1994

designed by Joanne Russ

ISBN 0 86469 218 8

Printed by the Dunmore Printing Company Ltd, Palmerston North

Contents

Schoolboys admire the engine as a bustle of passenger business proceeds on the platform, Oamaru 1938.

Introduction

New Zealand's extensive railway network dominated the country's transport services for nearly fifty years, a period that coincided with the golden age of the steam locomotive. These engines, and the trains they hauled, were an integral part of New Zealand life. They provided inter-city transport for businessmen or politicians, a trip to town for housewives, and transport for commuters. Children went to school on local trains, families went on holiday by train, and sports teams travelled by train.

As in the pioneer days of air travel, the railway station was an important place in our towns and cities, with newspapers, mail and even milk supplies being carried by train. But the railway not only linked communities together, it provided employment as well — some 25,000 people were on the payroll of New Zealand Railways in 1955.

The first public railway line in New Zealand was opened on 1 December 1863 linking Christchurch and Ferrymead, four miles away. Other small lines were opened around the country but it was not until the public works policy of Julius Vogel came into effect in the 1870s that major progress was made.

By 1879 there were 1,136 miles of railway line in the country, and the line from Christchurch to Invercargill was complete. The length of line gradually increased until 1953 when it reached a peak of 3,558 miles. The completion of the North Island Main Trunk in 1908 was a major achievement, and linked the two sections of the North Island network.

More lines were added during the inter-war years. The completion of the Otira tunnel in 1923 linked Westland to the South Island network. In the north, Auckland was linked to Whangarei in 1925, and to Tauranga in 1928. The line to Gisborne was completed in 1942. By 1945, when the

Christchurch-Picton line was opened, the New Zealand rail system was virtually complete.

As well as increasing the length of line, the Railways Department was constantly improving its facilities and the services offered. The workshops at Petone, Hillside and elsewhere kept up with the latest technology in both engines and carriages. Various innovations were tried, including dining cars and 'Ladies' cars. The premier expresses — the Main Trunk and the South Express — were well up to international standards, with the South Express in particular being noted for its elegance during its heyday.

The rise of alternative means of transport, as well as coal shortages at a crucial time after the Second World War created a gradual decline in passenger rail transport. The technological development of buses, cars and aircraft had been so speeded up by wartime demands that they were now able to take over as the main methods of transport in New Zealand. Today's Railways Corporation runs its passenger routes primarily as a subsidized social service, and maintains few inter-city trains (it has its own bus fleet for long and short distance passenger transport) and now concentrates on the more profitable area of freight transport.

Opposite: Beyond Sawyers Bay Junction the mainline north out of Dunedin takes off on a long curving embankment to begin the gruelling climb past Upper Port Chalmers and up the Mihiwaka Bank, culminating in the ultimate ordeal of the grim Mihiwaka Tunnel. This is a passenger's-eye-view of No. 174 Invercargill-Lyttleton Express sweeping through the junction. It was taken in 1938 from the second car as it leant hard against the outer rail of the curve, careering after the two fast moving engines (Wab and Ab). The two tracks on the right belong to the Port Chalmers Branch, the outer being the passing loop. Note the old time semaphore signals — three starters and three home signals. The mainline starter is in the off position. All this recalls vivid recollections of the muffled bumps and momentary lurching of the car bogies over the junction points. Before long, Otago Harbour will be out of sight, soon to be replaced by the magnificent panorama of Blueskin Bay.

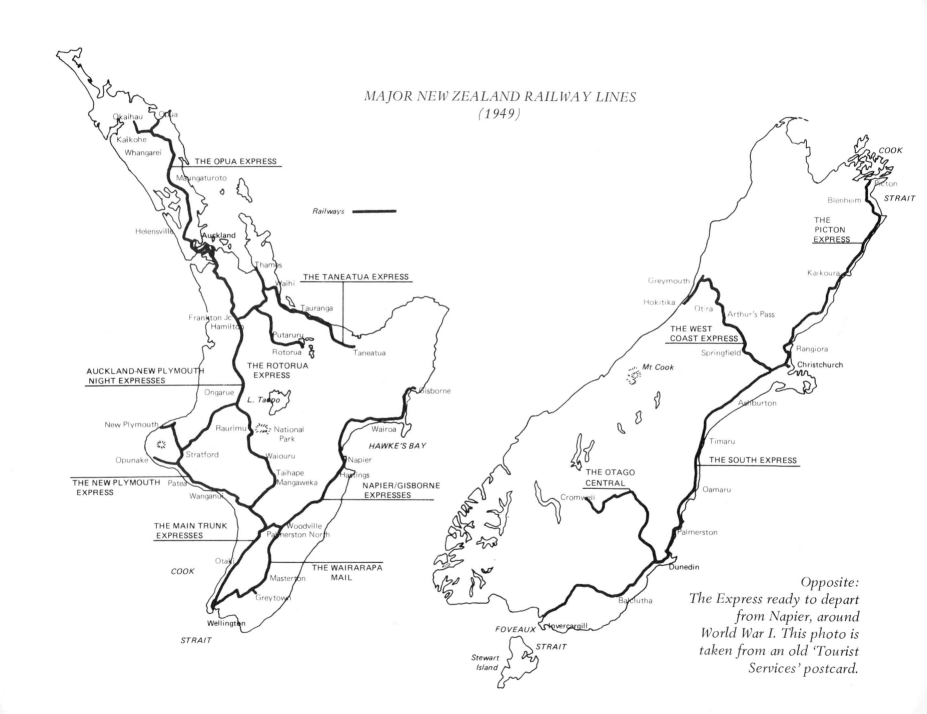

MAJOR NEW ZEALAND RAILWAY LINES
(1949)

Railways ────────

THE OPUA EXPRESS

Okaihau   Opua
Kaikohe
Whangarei
Maungaturoto
Helensville
Auckland
Thames
Waihi
Tauranga
THE TANEATUA EXPRESS
Frankton Jc
Hamilton
Putaruru
Rotorua
Taneatua
THE ROTORUA EXPRESS
AUCKLAND-NEW PLYMOUTH NIGHT EXPRESSES
Ongarue
L. Taupo
New Plymouth
Raurimu   National Park
Opunake
Stratford
Waiouru
THE NEW PLYMOUTH EXPRESS   Patea
Taihape
Mangaweka
Wanganui
Gisborne
Wairoa
HAWKE'S BAY
Napier
Hastings
NAPIER/GISBORNE EXPRESSES
THE MAIN TRUNK EXPRESSES
Woodville
Palmerston North
Otaki
COOK
Masterton
Greytown
THE WAIRARAPA MAIL
Wellington
STRAIT

COOK
STRAIT
Picton
Blenheim
THE PICTON EXPRESS
Kaikoura
Greymouth
Hokitika
Otira   Arthur's Pass
THE WEST COAST EXPRESS
Springfield
Rangiora
Christchurch
Mt Cook
Ashburton
Timaru
THE SOUTH EXPRESS
THE OTAGO CENTRAL
Cromwell
Oamaru
Palmerston
Dunedin
Balclutha
FOVEAUX   Invercargill
STRAIT
Stewart Island

*Opposite:
The Express ready to depart
from Napier, around
World War I. This photo is
taken from an old 'Tourist
Services' postcard.*

Part One: The North Island

The Opua Express

The scene at Auckland's old Queen Street railway station was much enlivened in December 1925 by the introduction of the Opua Express, serving Whangarei and the Bay of Islands, and with a section running up the Kaikohe branch to its terminus at Okaihau. Travelling some 180 miles from Auckland up through the hinterland of the Northland peninsula, the train had the distinction of being New Zealand's northernmost express, and added a completely new dimension to the Auckland district provincial services.

Throughout the steam era the Opua Express remained the chief railway passenger service to Northland, until it gave way to the diesel railcars in November 1956. But the railway passenger became a more and more elusive creature, and all railway passenger service to Northland came to an end in July 1967.

A trip on the Opua Express produced its own distinctive flavour of train travel experience. Northland is typically a countryside of tumbling bush-topped hills, with many curves, grades and tunnels. It has been claimed that there were more curves on the North line than any other main line in the country. However, there were only a few very sharp curves and good running was not unduly inhibited. The ruling grades over most of the route were one in 50 or 60, but oddly enough, the steepest climbs were in the Auckland suburban area, with a one in 39 from Newmarket to Mt Eden and a one in 36 from Swanson to Waitakere. These latter grades led to some very interesting banking engine arrangements at times of heavy loading. Some of the grades led up to tunnels through confronting ridges. There were as many as twelve tunnels in all, the longest being the 1,982 ft Golden Stairs between Paparoa and Meretu.

An unusual aspect of the line was that its bigger bridges all crossed over inlets of the sea rather

Ja 1278 working the morning train from Helensville through Kingsland in October 1965. This was one of Auckland's last regular steam passenger trains.

than rivers as such. The longest of them, and a very imposing structure, was the Otamatea 'River' Bridge, an old-style timber truss of seventeen spans, crossing an inlet of the Kaipara Harbour at Ranganui, eighty-six miles from Auckland. Riding over this bridge was one of the more memorable moments of the run. The remains of the old wharf could be seen below the train, and the waterway with its mangrove fringes was a sight which belonged so much to the North.

At Newmarket junction, near the beginning of its run, the Opua Express traversed a very odd stretch of track, unique on any New Zealand main line. This was the famous Newmarket Triangle, a relic from the days of pioneer railway construction. The Triangle was, in effect, a reversing loop whereby trains for the north could move out of Newmarket without becoming reversed in the process. A northbound train would back out of the station onto a long dead-end spur track, then it would move forward again around a curve in the direction of Mt Eden. On occasions when a train was too long for the spur (i.e. when it exceeded nine cars) it would come up from Auckland with the cars set up in reverse, and would then leave Newmarket in the correct order, taking a direct curve on to the Mt Eden line. This was known as 'The Old Road'. The two curves and the line at their base created a form of triangle, hence the popular name of 'Newmarket Triangle'.

Although the North line was not opened throughout until 1925, segments of it had roots deep in the history of the area. At the south end the Helensville-Kumeu section formed part of the so-called 'Portage Railway' from Helensville (Kaipara steamers) to Riverhead (for the Auckland steamers) opened in October 1875. This line used to be worked by the strange-looking B class double-ended Fairlie engines hauling four-wheeled passenger cars. This arrangement lasted until Kumeu was connected by rail with Auckland in July 1881.

At the north end, a segment from Kawakawa to Taumarere was opened as early as February 1877. By 1911 there was a line through from Opua to the port of Whangarei at Onerahi, four miles south of Whangarei. The link to Onerahi crossed Whangarei harbour (or the Hatea River) by means of an impressive lift span bridge (the only one ever on the NZR). The bridge became popularly known as the 'Gullroost' on account of the attachment that the local seagulls had for it. Boat trains ran from Opua to Onerahi to connect with the afternoon steamer for Auckland, the train comprising a highly polished Baldwin 2-6-2 tank engine (Wb class) and a rather motley collection of 6-wheeler and 44 ft bogie cars. All this disappeared with the inauguration of the through express to Auckland, and the bridge was dismantled after the closing of the Onerahi line in 1933.

Throughout the years of steam passenger travel to the North the Opua Express was worked

A lively scene at Otiria junction one afternoon in January 1953 after the arrival of the Auckland-Opua Express. Some people are hurrying to catch bus connections to the far north while others are coping with the pangs of travel hunger in the refreshment rooms in the foreground. Shortly, No. 15 will be split in two at the further end of the 56 ft composite car in the foreground. The front end of the train will continue on to Opua, while the rest will run in the opposite direction up the Kaikohe branch.

The Auckland-Opua Express skims over the Whangarei City sky-line as it continues its northbound journey on a showery afternoon in 1950. The cars parked outside the Grand Hotel and the reserve in the foreground help to fix the period of the photo.

The Express from Opua takes up an interesting stance at the sharp curve at Avondale while it drops some passengers (including the author) in the late afternoon sunshine on 28 June 1950. J-1213 is in a mid-state of undress with its streamlining still retaining the torpedo smoke box front. Wab-765 rushing in on a northbound suburban train at the opposite platform confirms that No. 50 is now working its way through the Auckland suburban area.

A group of youthful passengers on an excursion watch with rapt attention as a fireman prepares to couple up the approaching engine to the train. The massive tender end suggests a K class engine. The open-ended platform with its cage like railings and gates, for so long the vogue in NZR car design, provides an excellent vantage point for the purpose. The wide end of the wooden-bodied car distinguishes it as one of those specially built for the North Island Main Trunk express service from its inception in 1908.

first by Ab class engines (up to 1940), and from then on by the various versions of the J class engines until the end of the train in 1956. At busy times when extra power was needed it was the usual practice to double head the J engine with an Ab, so the long association of this class of engine with the train did not cease entirely.

Until 1940 the train was equipped with the standard 50 ft wooden mainline type car widely used on provincial expresses throughout New Zealand in the 1920s and 1930s. The normal make-up was about seven of these cars with matching guard's vans at either end for the separation at Otiria Junction.

TIMETABLE AUCKLAND-OPUA EXPRESS 1943

HASL	M	Stations	No. 15 Daily	No. 50 Daily
11	—	Auckland	dep 8.40 a.m.	arr 5.29 p.m.
11	38	Helensville (R)	dep 10.21 a.m.	dep 3.51 p.m.
131	90	Maungaturoto (R)	dep 12.31 p.m.	dep 1.41 p.m.
109	108	Waiotira Jc	dep 1.24 p.m.	dep 12.43 p.m.
		(Change for Dargaville Branch)		
13	130	Whangarei (R)	arr 2.15 p.m.	dep 11.48 a.m.
			dep 2.25 p.m.	arr 11.38 a.m.
96	172	Otiria Jc (R)	dep 4.25 p.m.	dep 9.51 a.m.
		(Kaikohe/Okaihu section detached/attached here)		
11	183	Opua*	arr 5.05 p.m.	dep 9.00 a.m.

(Connects with launches for Russell via Paihia)*
(R = refreshment station)

Opposite:
A celebrated oddity of Northland is the railway which runs down the main street of Kawakawa. The line is the Opua-Whangarei mainline and trains leaving or arriving at Kawakawa run right down the centre of Gillies Street, the main shopping street of the town, from one end to the other. There is no separation whatever of rail or road, the rails being recessed into the street like tram tracks, and traffic and trains mingle freely with each other in a delightful informality. This intriguing arrangement had its origins in an early line built in 1868 to carry coal from a mine in Kawakawa to the sea at Taumarere a mile or two away.

The North line was a delightful railway in many ways. As a train approached Auckland through the western suburbs it was rather like a roller coaster ride for passengers. From the Whau Creek at the beginning of the Auckland isthmus, eight miles from Auckland, it climbed to two summits at Mt Albert and Mt Eden stations before it fell again to sea level on the Waitemata. This contour was combined with an incessantly sharp curvature to make it even move interesting. On still afternoons the echoes of No. 50 blasting up the grade to Mt Albert, and up through Kingsland to Mt Eden could be heard for miles. Then there were the stations with their high signal boxes and signalling apparatus right out of the Victorian era railway catalogue. Towards the end of 1940, with considerable newspaper publicity, the train was re-equipped with the 56-ft steel panelled cars which were then coming off the assembly line at the Otahuhu workshops in considerable numbers. In addition to the standard first and second-class cars, which seated thirty-one and fifty-six passengers respectively, there were three composition versions which were exclusively built for this run. They accommodated fourteen first-class and twenty-eight second-class passengers, and were operated on the Kaikohe branch section of the train. This train set became dismantled during the war years, and in the post-war period the usual composition was as follows: Guard's van, 1908 Main Trunk wooden second-class, 1931 Main Trunk steel panel first-class, two 56 ft seconds, a 56 ft compo-car, 1908 Main Trunk wooden second-class, and guard's van. At this stage the leading van and first three cars ran on to Opua, while the rest ran to Okaikau. The reverse process operated in the south direction.

Memories of Nos 15 and 50

* I saw a good deal of the route of the train from the air while flying to Whangarei one day in the early 1950s in an N.Z.C. de Havilland 'Dominie' aircraft. The pilot, whom I know, invited me up front, and I enjoyed a marvellous view of the tortuous path of the line. It was fascinating enough watching its geometric precision in the rough country, but it was quite uncanny to see the way it disappeared from view altogether in the big tunnels under the ridges, emerging again at some considerable distance. I was lucky enough to see a goods train toiling along near Makarau, but it was much too early for the express.
* I encountered a news vendor, a survivor of the old days, selling his papers on No. 15 as late as 1950. Another tiny vignette was a tweedy countrywoman with a mail bag who always met the express at Mareretu, a lone figure who always had the little flag station to herself. I guessed she was the local postmistress and part of a declining system. Then there was a well-known guard on

The so-called Otamatea River bridge just north of Ranganui, which actually crosses a tidal arm of the Kaipara Harbour. For many years the trains used to charge over the bridge in good style to get a good run at the grade up through the Bickerstaffe tunnel to Mangaturoto, but speed was restricted in the bridge's later years because of deterioration in its structure. The photo shows a Ja engine crossing the bridge in 1965 when working a Railway Enthusiasts Special up to Portland.

Below:

On a sunny spring day in 1950 the Opua-Auckland Express pauses for a few minutes at Waiotira junction to pick up passengers from the Dargaville branch connection. The latter train has, as well, a large number of woolly coated passengers in J class stock wagons destined for the Westfield Freezing Works on a following goods train.

the express who when he retired started another career and became a celebrated character as a tour guide on the famous 'cream trip' around the Bay of Islands. He was popularly known as 'Kewpie' and had tourist launches named after him.

* The crossing of the Otamatea River at Ranganui has already been remarked upon. There were several reminders of the Kaipara Harbour to be seen from the train. The wharf structures adjoining the station yards at Helensville were another. A little-known relic of the Kaipara steamer days was the flag station at Mt Rex, 2 miles north of Helensville, which was very unusual in having a ticket window in its side wall, through which train tickets were dispensed for the special trains run from Helensville to meet the Dargaville steamer when it tied up at the Mt Rex wharf to suit the tide.

* An interesting trip incident always was the crossing of the two expresses at the small tablet station of Taipuha 100 miles north of Auckland at just after 1 p.m. The train crews changed over here in a time-honoured ritual, and one enjoyed the colourful sight of the passengers in the opposing express as it passed by. No. 15 usually arrived in advance and took the loop, with No. 50 showing up from the North within minutes as a rule and continuing on the main.

* No. 50's fast running along the miles of level and straight going between Kaukapakapa and Mt Rex, after the long spell of more or less constant hill country running south of Whangarei; No. 50 literally bounded along this stretch, and Helensville seemed to be reached in no time.

* In some contrast, but also memorable, was No. 15's climb up to the long Waitangi Tunnel (1,881 ft) north of Kanohi, seven miles out of Helensville. Beyond the station the line rose abruptly, the engine exhaust became more urgent, and soon we looked down on the landscape. Suddenly scrub and fern seemed to close in on the train and the next moment the car plunged into a very dark, narrow tunnel with its brick walls only a matter of inches away.

A photo from the mid-1920s showing the new Auckland-Wellington Daylight Limited making a spirited departure from Auckland's old downtown terminal behind the Chief Post Office. Its glistening Ab engine has all the stops open, and appears to be floating out of the city on a cushion of steam. This was the high tide in the Main Trunk express service with three daily expresses to Wellington. The 'Daylight' introduced a new dimension to the previously night-oriented service. But it was to suffer many vicissitudes, and it is only with the introduction of the new Silver Fern railcars that a permanent daylight service seems to be assured.

In the heyday of the steam passenger train, the Prime Minister, like everyone else, rode the rails, usually in one of the special ministerial cars kept in each island. These cars were always beautifully turned out, staffed by selected attendants, and generally attached to the rear of express and mail trains. Sometimes the trip down the line would be used as a convenient opportunity for 'politicking', addressing electors on station platforms en route. This photo appeared in the Auckland Weekly News on 29 October 1925 and shows 'the Hon. J.G. Coates and Mrs Coates at Newmarket as they left for their election tour.'

1: The Main Trunk Expresses

The Main Trunk Express, linking Auckland and Wellington, became the premier passenger operation in New Zealand from its inauguration in 1909. Until the present ascendency of highway and airway, the expresses handled the mainstream of travel between these centres: businessmen and holidaymakers, footballers and politicians, civil servants and bushmen, family people and all the others. If the Governor-General went north for a state occasion in Auckland the vice-regal car would be coupled to the rear of one of the expresses. Similarly with the Prime Minister and other VIPs. Night after night, year in and year out, a heavy flow of people moved up and down the North Island in these long trains.

Comparisons between the North Island and South Island trunk expresses are inevitable. The South Express tended to project a more elegant and polished image; it was more a train with a tradition and reflected something of the ordered and mature countryside through which it ran. Although famed for its speed exploits on the Canterbury Plains, it was a train with origins in a more spacious age. By contrast, the Main Trunk expresses were more urgent, businesslike, and always travel-stained. They were trains of the twentieth century. The harsher environment through which they operated often left its mark on them.

My earliest memories of the Trunk expresses in 1929-30 recall visions of flexing, gliding monsters materialising out of the smoke at Thorndon, breathing awesome exhausts from the double-heading locomotives as they laboured up the steep grade beyond the Hutt Road and were swallowed up in a tight single-track tunnel bored through the hills encircling Wellington. There was nothing to match it: the tumultuous racket, soon followed by silence with pungent smoke quietly billowing out of the empty tunnel mouth. This was the old Wellington and Manawatu

Railway Company route out of Wellington; there was much less drama when it was replaced by the Tawa Flat deviation in 1937.

The collective experience of Main Trunk travel surely creates a special chapter in the story of 'going places' in New Zealand. To many it was a 'sleepless ordeal', others recall a 'wake-up-at-all-stops' doze, while there was a seasoned minority who claimed to sleep through it all, oblivious,

A sleeping berth avoided much of the wear and tear for those who could afford it, but a first-class reclining seat made life more tolerable than the spartan straight-backed seats of the second class. Even with the train enthusiast there was a kind of love-hate relationship with night train travel. Without question it was a wearisome ride in the day cars for most people; all night long they sought elusive comfort with the NZR pillow. Riding was often hard on the sharp curves in the high country; sometimes the steam heat was too hot or too cold, while the intrusions of smoke, cinders and dust built up a bleary 'morning after' effect.

In retrospect, there were compensations which loom larger than the drawbacks: the sense of involvement in the train's progress and the busy activity on the line, the remote railway towns of the Trunk occurring like brightly lit oases in the void, the big refreshment stations, the native forests brooding in the moonlight, and the elusive glimpse of a mountain stream in the night. Once, I saw Ngaruahoe in a fiery eruption through a window of No. 227, a sight never to be forgotten, with the mountain seeming only a mile or two away. Another time, early in the diesel age, I was dozing in a sleeper on the Limited when I heard the whistle of a steam helper boosting the Da diesel on its climb up the Spiral. It was an eerie sensation, a ghostly sound from the past, echoing through the dark night. One recalls such compensations as the exhilarating run of No. supplemented by numerous relief expresses at holiday times. For a short time there were also bound along the long tangents into Paekakariki, to that scenic coast in its summer and winter guises from where you could see the South Island, followed by the more tranquil Paramata Harbour, and that triumphal moment when the train suddenly bursts out of Tawa No. 1 Tunnel into full view of Wellington Harbour — surely one of the most dramatic moments the NZR had to offer. There were also things like a pair of Ka's backing int an express at Taumarunui at holiday time; the exuberant acceleration out of town; the awesome feel of tremendous power on the grade beyond Kakahi. I once knew a train buff who, when he had nothing better to do during the weekend, would take a train ride down to Taumaranui and back on the respective expresses which crossed near there. He found the rhythm and 'world-apartness' of the train soothing to the spirit.

The regular express service on the Main Trunk began on 14 February 1909. It superseded a

Opposite:
An appealing NZR advertisement. The reality may have been something less for many passengers, but for others the evocation is authentic.

rail and steamer route between Auckland and Wellington via New Plymouth. For all their importance, the Main Trunk expresses came thirty-one years after the South expresses. But what they
lacked in history they were soon able to make up in volume of passenger traffic. Before long, two
trains were needed, and a basic pattern of service was established, with two overnight trains
supplemented by numerous relief expresses at holiday times. For a short time there were also
daytime expresses. Connections with the inter-island ferry to Lyttleton were an important con-
sideration in these timetables.

The initial northbound express departed at 11.45 a.m. and arrived at 6.58 a.m. The Southbound departed at 9.15 p.m. and arrived at 4.25 p.m., with a journey time of 19¼ hours. In the
last years of steam the Limited did the run in 14¼ hours. Over the years various adjustments were
made to the timetables. The first was the addition of the second express in 1914 and the cutting
of the journey time to 17 h 45 min. At Auckland the departure times were 12.40 p.m. and 8.50
p.m.; at Wellington, 1.10 p.m. and 9.10 p.m.

Probably the most important development in steam was the inauguration of the Night Limited
expresses in December 1924. This was a prestige title borrowed from world-famous trains such as
The Twentieth Century Limited of the New York Central Railroad in the U.S.A. Essentially,
a 'Limited' was designed to move passengers at all possible speed by slashing stops and limiting
loads. The Night Limited cut 3 h 45 min off the run in one swoop, largely by reducing stops
from fifteen to six (Frankton, Taumaranui, Ohakune, Taihape, Marton and Palmerston North).
Loads were initially restricted to a total of nine for the new Limiteds, but with the advent of the
heavier K engines in the 1930s the loads were raised as high as thirteen. The new Limited timetables were: Southbound, depart 7.10 p.m., arrive 9.31 a.m.; Northbound, depart 7.10 p.m.,
arrive 9.26 a.m. At this time the southbound express left Auckland at 7.45 p.m. and the northbound left Wellington at 12.40 p.m. (later this was changed to 2.00 p.m.).

By 1937 the ordinary expresses were given the long familiar 3.00 p.m. departure times, with an
ultimate journey time of sixteen hours. The departure time of the Limited was standardised at
7.15 p.m. at both terminals with journey times of 14¼ hours.

A notable event in the Main Trunk Express service was the introduction, in November 1925, of
a 15¼-hour Daylight Limited, which left Auckland at 8.00 a.m., but slack season patronage was
lacking and the service was discontinued in June 1926. The convenience of night travel continued
to appeal to most people. The Daylight was before its time as a regular service. Subsequently, it
ran only occasionally at Christmas and Easter, until September 1929 when it was again made into
a regular service (complete with the addition of lounge cars), only to be killed off by the De-

Inside an open saloon closed vestibule first-class car of 1931-32. These steel-sided cars were 50 ft long, 8 ft 11 in wide and carried twenty-nine passengers. Coloured, patterned moquette was used for seat upholstery for the first time. Fourteen cars of this type were built at the Otahuhu Workshops.

The first lounge cars used on the NZR were not on the Rotorua Limiteds as more popularly supposed, but on the Daylight Limiteds of 1929. These were standard wooden Main Trunk cars specially converted for the purpose. A charge of 75c over and above the first-class fare was made, and the cars were quite popular, until they became casualties with the Limited itself in 1930.

Opposite:
The scene the day after five cars of the Auckland-Wellington Express (Train No. 227) had been derailed by a washout at a point about two miles beyond Oio (20 m from Taumarunui) on the evening of 5 January 1945. No. 227 was carrying a big load of 400 passengers; it was holiday time, and there was still a lot of travel by service personnel. Air and road competition was as yet minimal. The train reached the point of the derailment at about 10.15 p.m., and the washout had scoured a gap about 20 ft deep under the track. Incredibly, the engine crossed the gap, but the five cars, as the photo shows, were derailed and spreadeagled about the embankment. None suffered any structural damange — a tribute to the strength of their construction — and only two passengers needed any medical attention. There is little doubt that slips were the main hazard of train operation in New Zealand, whether they were of the variety which caused large pieces of hillside to fall on the line, or washouts which caused segments of embankments to disappear and leaving rails sagging in space.

pression of 1930. Henceforth it reverted to holiday services until it was terminated in 1941 because of the war. Revived in 1949 as a Christmas and summer holiday service, it ran (as J-9 and J-10) until superseded by the diesel-hauled Scenic Daylight expresses.

Any account of the Main Trunk express services could scarcely omit some reference to the greatly swollen flow of passengers at Christmas and Easter, and the numerous extra trains used then, to handle it. It is likely that this reached a climax in 1939, when, on Easter Thursday, 6 April, no fewer than eight expresses were run between Auckland and Wellington in each direction.

A new 'Main Trunk' type of carriage had been specially built for the Main Trunk expresses. Of standard North Island 50 ft lengths, they were characterised by being wider (8 ft 9 in instead of 7 ft 10 in) and having single fascias with recessed platforms. First class seated thirty, second class forty-four at four abreast. They were divided into two saloons by the lavatory accommodation, and lighting was by Pintsch gas.

Sleeping cars were provided for the first time in New Zealand on this service, using the same basic design of vehicle. They contained twenty berths in six cabins. Later, a modified version was evolved, without open platforms, of eighteen berths in seven cabins. Naturally enough, the four berth cabins did not prove very popular with passengers.

Another interesting car produced for the new expresses was the dining car. Similar in length and outline to the other cars, they had closed vestibules, seated twenty-five diners and used gas for both lighting and cooking. The diners ran on the Main Trunk expresses until they were withdrawn in 1917 as a wartime stringency. They were never reinstated, but eight of them were converted into 'Ladies Cars' with additional toilet facilities.

This type of Main Trunk carriage stock was used exclusively in that service for nearly twenty-five years and made the expresses on the run immediately identifiable. Their wide overhang and stubby appearance were very distinctive features. In later years the NZR installed bellows connectors to improve passage between the open platforms of adjoining carriages.

No matching guard's vans were built to conform with the carriages. Standard 50 ft Vans of the Mainline type were used, as on other express trains.

Power for the new expresses was provided by New Zealand designed and built engines. For easier going there were the famous Addington A class 4-6-2s, surely among the most elegant of New Zealand locomotives, while at the same time being smooth-running and reliable. Our local locomotive engineers at the turn of the century were acquiring a reputation for the quality and appearance of their products. The A was considered their masterpiece, and the trunkline expresses hauled by them in both islands had now acquired a distinctive New Zealand look. For the mountain section between Taihape and Taumaranui, eighteen large X class 4-8-2 Mountain Type engines were built. They were looked upon as the monsters of their day and although the general

Opposite: For over fifty years the high and lonely places of the North Island echoed and reverberated with the passage of the steam expresses between Auckland and Wellington. Every night for a few fleeting moments farms, forests, gorges, and wastelands would be illuminated by the sweeping headlight beams of the locomotives in their headlong flight. For the last thirty-three years of the period the massive K class engines produced the action and seemed to be peculiarly at home in the rugged surroundings. Here, Ka-948 gets under way from National Park on 29 January 1965 shortly before the end of steam on the Main Trunk expresses. Although hundreds of passengers travelled up and down the Main Trunk every night of the year, this is an episode in the steam saga witnessed by very few people. Most passengers are asleep or dozing, and to the wakeful ones, National Park is no more than a name on an illuminated station window. When winter gales blew down from the slopes of Ruapehu lashing the trains, and making the steam and smoke billow and swirl low over the cars, the warm steam-heated interiors afforded a special feeling of comfort and security, and the muffled, melancholy blast of the engine somehow seemed reassuring. National Park (formerly Waimarino) was the station for Château Tongariro and the snow sports of Ruapehu. Over the years many snow enthusiasts left the expresses in the middle of the night, bound for the mountain. In pre-war days snow sports specials were run to National Park from Auckland and Wellington, but for many years now practically all this class of traffic has been by road.

Sometime soon after the accession of King George V in 1910 and prior to the outbreak of World War 1, the Main Trunk Express is seen drifting through Mataroa, six miles north of Taihape, like a stately procession or caravanserai led by a polished X class engine, Z class luggage van, postal van, Aa carriages, and guard's van. Today, Mataroa is no more.

Addington styling was used, they were very cumbersome-looking machines with large boilers perched high above small 3 ft 9 in diameter driving wheels. The small drivers gave them more power on the grades — they could pull a train nearly 50% heavier up the Raurimu Spiral — but this was at the cost of speed which was limited to 25 mph.

The A and X class engines worked the Main Trunk expresses, with some help from the Baldwin Aa class 4-6-2s of 1914 in the middle districts, until about the end of World War 1 when they were gradually superseded by the new and more powerful Ab class 4-6-2s and Wab class 4-6-4 tank engines, the latter like the Xs, being concentrated on the Taumarunui-Taihape section. The Ab engines, with fewer concessions to elegance than the A's, became the most numerous and familiar express engines in the country. Their cylindrical Vanderbilt tenders were a unique feature of the design. The Wab engines were in essence a tank engine version of the Ab, the side tanks being used to give them extra adhesion on the rails. Both these classes of engines, double-heading as needed, worked the Main Trunk expresses right through the 1920s until the 'Big Power' era when the huge K class 4-8-4s were introduced between 1932 and 1936. These handsome engines, based on the latest American designs, were about half as powerful again as the Ab's and could run a 500-ton passenger train at 64 mph. Thirty were built, and before long they were a familiar sight on the Main Trunk route.

It was a time for change, too, in passenger accommodation. In 1931-32 the old wooden cars used on both the Limited and the ordinary express were replaced by steel-panelled cars with curved sides and closed vestibules. They were 50 ft long and 8 ft 11 in wide, and were quite different inside with a single open saloon and toilets at each end of the car. They were adorned with the handsome NZR coat of arms on the enamelled car sides. In all, forty-two were built — fourteen first-class cars seating twenty-nine, and twenty-eight in second class, seating forty-four. The combination of K class engines and these new cars gave the Main Trunk expresses a thoroughly modern image. In retrospect, the 1930s are now seen as the highest point in the development of the steam express in New Zealand.

Sleeping cars were an essential amenity. In 1925 a new 56 ft sleeper (No. 1616) containing nine 2-berth cabins with the traditional wood sheathing was built and displayed at the Dunedin and South Seas Exhibition of 1925-26. In 1927 four similar cars containing eight 2-berth cabins and kitchenettes were built, these cars being a milestone in NZR coachbuilding in that they were the first to employ steel sheathing with curved body sides, which subsequently became the NZR standard. In 1933 two further cars of this type were built, but they were only 50 ft long and had no kitchenettes.

We come now to the final chapter in the story of Main Trunk passenger cars in the steam era. In 1937, for the first time, the NZR was able to design a standard express carriage suitable for running on the mainlines of both islands. They were the now very familiar 56 ft 'bullet' type cars distinguished by both their wrap-around high arch roofs coming right down to the upper line of the windows without a fascia and the exaggerated body bulge. A total of seventy-one were built: nineteen first class with thirty-one seats, and fifty-two second class with fifty-six seats. The first-class cars were very comfortable with 3-position armchair style seating and a new pressure ventilation system, but the cramped arrangement of the then obsolete straight-back throw-over Scarret seats in the second-class cars was very disappointing, and did little to make rail travel attractive to the overnight express passenger. As one well known American railroad executive remarked, 'The time had come when it was a job getting them into the train, not packing them in.' By 1940 both the Limited and the Three O'Clock expresses were fully made up with the new stock which matched well with the K class engines and produced images of imposing, well-rounded trains well up with the times, and it was always impressive to watch the bigger cars rolling in and out of the terminals.

In addition to the 56 ft day cars, eleven day-sleepers were built in 1938 to the new specifications. These cars contained five 2-berth cabins plus an 11-seat first-class saloon, but to meet new traffic demands they were rebuilt as full sleepers from 1942 onwards. These were the last sleeping cars of the steam era.

We also come to the last phases of steam power on the Main Trunk express services. The years 1939-50 saw the introduction of the Ka class 4-8-4s, refined and streamstyled versions of the K class. The Ka's mainly worked the expresses from Paekakariki to Taumarunui, and K's worked further north. Fast and free running engines, they have been reliably timed at speeds of nearly 70 mph in Main Trunk passenger service. The last years saw the use of the J class 4-8-2s and their later relatives, the North British Ja's of 1952, in use between Taumarunui and Auckland. These engines had no trouble running a 10-car express to schedule on this section and were actually preferred by many engine crews to the bigger 4-8-4s. However, the latter were needed for the bigger holiday season loads, and it is appropriate to note here that the last runs of both the Limiteds and the Expresses were pulled by Ka class locomotives.

So much then, for an overall outline of the history of the Main Trunk express service during the years of steam. Its popularity reached a zenith during this era, and coincidentally as steam went into decline so did the railway passenger business and the expresses with it. With the introduction of the Viscount aircraft, and later the Boeing 737 jets, the Main Trunk express passenger business crumbled away. Towards the end the trains had shrunk to minimum proportions of four day cars (two second-class smoking and non-smoking, and two first-class carriages), with a single sleeper on the express and two to three on the Limited. There was also a general decline from the old standards of train cleaning and maintenance. These loadings increased at holiday times to create some of the old atmosphere, but sadly for the purist a practice then developed of using the surplus engine power by adding numbers of bogie freight vans to the tails of both trains. To see the Limited arrive at Auckland with a number of these in tow was a disillusioning experience for those who had known the great days when the express train was Lord of the Rails. The end was ominously near, and came soon enough when the new General Motors Da class diesel electric engines were made available for the job of handling the expresses. The last steam-powered Limited ran on 28 April 1963, and the last steam-powered Expresses on 5 February 1965. For some years they had been the last steam-powered expresses left in the North Island.

AUCKLAND-WELLINGTON EXPRESS SERVICE 1939 — TIMETABLE

HASL ft	M miles	Stations	No. 227 Express Daily Exc Sun		No. 229 Limited Daily Exc Sat	No. 626 Express Daily Exc Sun		No. 688 Limited Daily Exc Sat
9	—	Auckland	dep 3.00 p.m.		7.15 p.m.	arr 7.00 a.m.		9.30 a.m.
123	85	Frankton Jc (R)	arr 5.34 p.m.		9.29 p.m.	dep 4.30 a.m.		7.10 a.m.
			dep 5.45 p.m.		9.40 p.m.	arr 4.20 a.m.		6.50 a.m.
561	174	Taumaranui (R)	arr 9.08 p.m.		12.37 a.m.	dep 1.10 a.m.		4.03 a.m.
			dep 9.16 p.m.		12.45 a.m.	arr 1.00 a.m.		3.55 a.m.
1450	265	Taihape (R)	arr 1.30 a.m.		4.27 a.m.	dep 9.00 p.m.		12.28 a.m.
			dep 1.38 a.m.		4.35 a.m.	arr 8.52 p.m.		12.20 a.m.
100	339	Palmerston North(R)	dep 4.19 a.m.		6.55 a.m.	dep 5.46 p.m.		9.51 p.m.
			dep 4.29 a.m.		7.04 a.m.	arr 5.36 p.m.		9.41 p.m.
8	426	Wellington	arr 7.00 a.m.		9.30 a.m.	dep 3.00 p.m.		7.15 p.m.

(Highest station on line is Waiouru 2,670 ft. 241 miles from auckland)

(R = refreshment station)

*Holiday-time passengers in December 1946 boarding Train No. 322 (Taneatua-Auckland Express)
at the distinctive kiosk style station on the Strand at Tauranga. This station on the waterfront
was much more convenient than the main station on the north outskirts of town and was widely
used by passengers who had been shopping in town or by holidaymakers to and from the Mount
Maunganui ferry wharf which was adjacent. No. 322 has long since disappeared down the line for
the last time, and so too have the faceless railcars which superseded it. The Strand Station has
since been put to other uses.*

The Taneatua Express

The Taneatua Express provided the main passenger service from Auckland to the Bay of Plenty from 1928, when the Taneatua line was opened, until 1959 when the express was replaced by railcars. It never enjoyed the popularity of the Rotorua Express, partly because of the very circuitous route via Hamilton and Paeroa. However, it was a varied and interesting train ride, especially through the Karangahake and Athenree gorges, and along the shores of Tauranga Harbour. It was a long ride, too, nine miles further than from Christchurch to Dunedin. For the last sixty miles from Tauranga to Taneatua the express became an all-stations local, taking nearly three hours for this stretch. It was a good way to see the country at close quarters and absorb the local colour.

A novel feature of the operation of the Taneatua Express was the reversal it underwent at Paeroa Junction. The lines from Auckland and the Bay of Plenty converged on Paeroa Junction in the form of an inverted V, with the result that the down Taneatua Express became reversed at Paeroa and completed its journey to Taneatua with the guard's van next to the engine. Likewise, the up express left Taneatua in the orthodox fashion, but arrived in Auckland with the van next to the engine. In July 1959 the reversal was avoided by a direct line by-passing the town to the south, but the express had already given way to the railcars.

It is interesting to reflect that the Taneatua Express had a life of just over thirty years, ten more than its predecessor, the Thames Express. However, in the post-war years it suffered the same vicissitudes as the Rotorua Express, finishing up with a token service of two trains per week each way from 1951 onwards. It was a hopeless situation and in the final years it often operated in the off periods with as few as three carriages in its make-up. The Paeroa-Pokeno deviation upon which work had already started before World War II would have made a great difference to the success of the Taneatua Express had the line been completed in the 1920s. With the preoccupation with highways that developed after the war, this scheme was quietly dropped from the programme of railway works although a fair amount of formation had already been built.

The 1959 Auckland-Tauranga-Te Puke railcar substitutes for the Taneatua Express had a short life, being withdrawn in September 1967. The years of the locust had taken their toll. Notwithstanding the fact that the population of the Tauranga urban area (which includes Mt Maunganui) had risen to 30,000, the railcars were not carrying much more than a busload of passengers during non-holiday times. Railway passenger services to the Bay died with scarcely a murmur from the public.

Below is a summary of the 1939 timetable of the Taneatua Express, which is more or less typical:

TIMETABLE – AUCKLAND-TANEATUA EXPRESS 1939

HASL	M	Stations	No. 121 Daily	No. 322 Daily
11	–	Auckland	dep 9.08 a.m.	arr 6.20 p.m.
124	85	Frankton Jc (R)	arr 12.04 p.m.	dep 3.16 p.m.
			dep 12.26 p.m.	arr 3.08 p.m.
17	129	Paeroa Jc (R)	dep 2.21 p.m.	dep 1.20 p.m.
		(Change for Thames Branch)		
13	179	Tauranga (R)	arr 4.41 p.m.	dep 10.58 a.m.
			dep 4.51 p.m.	arr 10.47 a.m.
52	239	Taneatua*	arr 7.50 p.m.	dep 7.45 a.m.

(* Road connections to Opotiki and Gisborne)
(R = refreshment station)

The Auckland-Taneatua Express on the impressive steel truss bridge across Tauranga Harbour. This bridge, built in 1924 linking Tauranga with Matapihi on the other side of the harbour, is the longest in Auckland Province. It comprises 14 large 104 ft spans (1,456 ft) and has a long embankment leading up to it on the east side as well. The smoke billowing through the trusses denotes the Ab class locomotive hard at work on the front of the train.

It is about 12.50 p.m. and the Taneatua-Auckland Express has run around the shore of Tauranga Harbour from one end to the other. It has climbed the 3-mile Athenree Gorge with its 1 in 50 grade, stopped at Waihi, and is now traversing the crowded Karangahape Gorge through which the line runs between Waikino and Karangahape.

The Rotorua Express

T he Rotorua Express was the first express train in the Auckland province. It began running in 1894, and operated for sixty-five years until replaced by diesel railcars in 1959. Some of Rotorua's mana as a tourist centre rubbed off on the train, as holidaymakers from all over New Zealand travelled on it to see the sights of the 'Thermal Wonderland'. Certainly it was a train more closely associated with holidays and holiday travel than any other New Zealand express train.

Originally, the express service was a sketchy affair of one train a week, hauled by J class 2-6-0 engines and L class 2-4-0 tank engines with trains of old 44 ft wooden clerestory roof carriages, one of which was a very plushy 'birdcage' car. Time for the 171-mile journey was a leisurely 8 hr 40 min. Train loads were restricted – the L's took only sixty-five tons up the steep Mamaku grades, and the J's eighty tons.

In 1902 a full-scale daily express service was established with more advanced equipment both in locomotives and carriages. By this time the Baldwin Q class 4-6-2s and N class 2-6-2s (second series) had arrived on the scene from the United States and the more modern arch roof cars of the late 1890s appeared in the train's make-up. These were soon followed by the first (narrow window) and second (wide window) series of the 50 ft 'standard' wooden-bodied cars which were built at the Petone workshops soon after the beginning of the century. In December 1903, new 44 ft dining cars were incorporated into the train. A former Main Trunk guard Percy Bunting recalls them:

'I well remember as a boy the excellent dining car service on the Rotorua Express. The dining car was picked up at Mercer on the down trip in a very slick shunting operation, and placed in

Opposite:
Ja-1283, built by the North British Locomotive Company of Glasgow in 1951, photographed at the head of the Rotorua-Auckland Express at Mercer in August 1954. The North British Ja's were readily distinguished by their butterfly-style headlights and were a very popular sight on Auckland District passenger trains in the closing stages of the steam era.

the middle of the train, after which luncheon was served. The car was later dropped at Putaruru after serving afternoon tea.' This facility was withdrawn in July 1917, a casualty of World War I.

An important event in the evolution of engine power was the introduction of the A class 4-6-2 compounds around 1910. These engines were recognised as masterpieces of Edwardian elegance; the magnificence of their brass work and the high standard of polish made them a sight to behold. With this increased power and a typical string of the latest 'mainline' cars in their olive green paint and yellow trim, the Rotorua Express had become quite an imposing train. By 1914 the speed limit on the route was raised to 45 mph, and for a time a 7 hr schedule was maintained. During and after World War I there were cutbacks, and at one stage the train was combined with the Thames Express at Morrinsville.

Another significant change in motive power came in the early 1920s with the advent of the famous Ab class 4-6-2s. Before long they were largely standard power on most of the provincial expresses as well as on the main trunk lines. The journey time of the Rotorua Express was cut to 6 hr 40 min, and these engines were to be identified with the train for the next two decades. Railway passenger business continued to boom and the express was often built up to as many as ten or twelve carriages, and more at holiday periods. During this period numbers of the third series of 50 ft wooden body 'mainline' cars were incorporated in the make-up, but interestingly enough one of the quaint 'birdcage' cars of earlier times continued to run on the train to provide compartment-type accommodation.

In 1930 there was a real revolution in passenger equipment with the introduction of luxurious steel panelled cars with enclosed vestibules and bellows connections. The cars were specially built for the service, and were the first of their kind in New Zealand. There was even an observation-lounge car at the rear of the train, in the best tradition of the famous American expresses of the time. The first-class cars carried twenty-nine passengers and the second-class forty-six. They were handsome with a gleaming baked enamel red finish, and the NZR coat of arms emblazoned on the sides. The train was given the prestige title of 'Rotorua Limited' and the journey time was reduced to six hours. Unfortunately, the new train was not the success it deserved to be. The advent of the Great Depression in 1930 curtailed holiday travel, as at the same time road competition was increasing. The observation car only lasted for a few months, and the Depression make-up of the train was often no more than four cars and a van. As conditions improved, the normal make-up increased to five or seven cars. With the coming of World War II, and petrol rationing and travel of service personnel, the patronage of the express was boosted to record heights.

Train No. 288, Rotorua-Auckland Express, labours up the Tarukenga Bank on the eastern slopes of the Mamakus in October 1955. The engine is J-1235, and the vertical exhaust indicates the very moderate speed. In the far background of the spacious landscape Lake Rotorua can be dimly seen below the encircling hills. This was the mecca of countless tourists who travelled to Rotorua in the heyday of the Rotorua Express.

It is shortly before 3 p.m. at Putaruru one day in 1950. The J class engine working No. 133 has refilled its tender at the brick water tower in preparation for the gruelling climb ahead to the summit of the Mamakus, and it is now backing to its train again. Here we have a vignette of railway operation as old as railways. A shunter is waiting alongside the vestibule connection of the leading car to signal the driver as he backs up, and attend to the re-coupling of engine and car. The couplers here are of the automatic kind, but the air and steam heating hoses have to be connected up again by hand. In the background through the narrowing gap can be seen the striking torpedo boiler front of another J class engine in the loop at the head of a Rotorua bound goods train.

The Rotorua Limited departing old Queen Street Station.
A total Limited in charge of a highly polished Ab engine threads its way out of the old downtown station which was closed down in November 1930. The new Rotorua Limiteds were introduced in May 1930, so the photo was taken in the intervening period. It is noted that the splendid observation car has already been taken off the train, to be replaced by a guard's van occupying its normal place. Downtown city buildings provide a unique background, and illustrate the close identity between the city and the old station.

1910 Super-Power.
An impressively cylindered A Compound, not long out of the erecting shops, leaves the downtown Auckland terminal for Rotorua with the Express in 1910. Tourists on the Express will be well rewarded if they see geyser activity to surpass the smoke effects created by the Compound in leaving town.

AUCKLAND – FRANKTON JC – ROTORUA (Weekdays)

HASL	M	Stations	Rotorua Limited		Rotorua Limited	
8	–	Auckland	dep	10.10 a.m.	arr	4.00 p.m.
21	43	Mercer (R)	arr	11.28	dep	2.38
			dep	11.33	arr	2.33
123	85	Frankton Jc (R)	arr	12.41	dep	1.23
			dep	1.02	arr	1.01
131	86	Hamilton	dep	1.10	dep	12.57
88	102	Morrinsville Jc	arr	1.40	dep	12.22
			dep	1.43	arr	12.17
531	139	Putaruru (R)	arr	2.47	dep	11.17 a.m.
			dep	2.55	arr	11.10
938	171	Rotorua	arr	4.15	dep	10.00 a.m.

(R) = Refreshment Station

After two decades of solid, reliable service, the time had come for the Ab engines to give way to more modern and more powerful replacements. At the beginning of the war the big K class 4-8-4s took over the run and handled the heavier passenger loads with little difficulty, including the climbs over the Mamakus. But, before long, the streamlined J class 4-8-2s built in Britain in 1940 were doing the job, and continued on until the latter years of the train when the Ja's were also used. Improved power performance is reflected in the maximum load figures on the Mamakus. Whereas the A and Ab classes were limited to 150 tons and 170 tons respectively, the figures for the K and J classes were 260 tons and 210 tons. (Of course, double heading was practised when needed. An intriguing example of double heading took place on the inaugural run of the Rotorua Limited in 1930 when the Ab train engine was assisted up the west side of the Mamakus by a Q class engine of 1901. One always enjoyed these little incongruities of the NZR.)

The last depressing phase of the Rotorua Express came after the war. It began with drastic coal cuts in 1944 reducing the service to three trains per week. In 1951 further cuts reduced the trains to two per week, a mere token timetable. The once beautiful carriages fell into a state of neglect while more and more new buses appeared on the highway. Soon there were as many as five or six buses per day competing with the train and taking only a little over five hours for the trip. The drop in the railway passenger business was calamitous. In 1929 35,554 tickets had been sold at Rotorua, and in 1939, 33,242 — but in 1959 the figure had fallen to a mere 6,342. Finally, the Rotorua Express gave up the ghost in 1959, and was replaced by diesel railcars. But even these could not stem the drift, and the railway passenger service to Rotorua was abandoned in 1968 after an eventful history of seventy-five years.

Some Rotorua Line Memories:

* The great 1-in-35 climbs up both sides of the Mamakus, the steepest and most sustained mainline grades on the NZR. It was a 9-mile climb on the Rotorua side from Ngongotaha, and a 16-mile climb on the Putaruru side from Pinedale. On the eastbound run in particular, it was stirring to hear the bark of the engine exhaust reverberating against the jagged rock cuttings as it fought its way up every inch of the grade. Mr T.A. McGavin of the *New Zealand Railway Observer* recorded a fine effort on Easter Monday 1956 when Jb-1239 worked a six total express on 145 tons out of Putaruru. The timetable allowed 55 mins for the 18.3 miles up to Mamaku including a stop at Ngatira. No. 1239 covered the distance in 39½ min with a 1½ min stop at Ngatira thrown in. A speed of well over 20 mph must have been maintained up the 1-in-35 grade, a very fine performance.
* The run in the reverse direction, from Mamaku to Pinedale, was in my experience one of the most exhilarating train rides on the NZR. With the combination of steep fall, easy alignment and good track, the express always seemed to fly down the grade, but with a most satisfying and reassuring train motion.
* Ngatira, the intermediate tablet station on the western slope, was a lonely outpost in the mountains and a tiny level kink in an otherwise sustained 1-in-35 grade. The grade simply rose out of the east end of the station yard. While travelling on the 4.30 p.m. Rotorua-Frankton passenger train in 1943, I recall the crossing of a long troop special standing in the wide loop with two K engines on the head end. There was not an inch to spare!

The highlight of the 171-mile Auckland-Rotorua run was undoubtedly the 27-mile section over the Mamakus between Putaruru (139 m) and Ngongotaha (166 m). Remnants of majestic native forest, and a dramatic first glimpse of Lake Rotorua from high up on the eastern descent, were notable scenic attractions, but from the railway point of view special interest lay in the 18-mile climb from the west at 1 in 35 to the summit at Mamaku (1890 ft above sea level) followed by a 9-mile descent also at 1 in 35 to the shores of the lake at Ngongotaha. The climb up the western slope was easily the steepest sustained mainline gradient in New Zealand.

Rotorua Express on Parnell Bank
A racy-looking Baldwin N class 2-6-2 of 1901 climbs the old single track line to Newmarket with the Rotorua Express in 1903. As well as the engine, the cars are also quite new: the third and fourth are American compartment cars of 1900, and the other locally built cars would only be a year or two older. At this time the Q's were also in service on the Rotorua Express out of Auckland, and it is assumed that the N was rostered for the run on this occasion because of the light loading.

* The first glimpse of Lake Rotorua on the eastbound trip after breaking out of the forest was always a dramatic moment.

* Putaruru, the afternoon tea stop for No. 133 and the headquarters of the erstwhile Taupo-Totara Timber Co.'s seventy-mile bush line to Mokai. Their line was on the opposite side of the platform, and I consider myself fortunate to have seen the company's 2-4-4-2 Mallet locomotive, built by the American Locomotive Co., simmering there. This engine has been beautifully restored, and today it is the main attraction on the Glenbrook Vintage Railway south of Auckland.

* The fast running over the Hauraki Plains beyond Morrinsville junction through Matamata to Tirau, passed through some of the nicest farming country in the province. Mr McGavin recorded a run here on No. 133 at Easter 1941 when J-1209 with a twelve total was running 12 min. late out of Morrinsville. He said: 'the acceleration out of Morrinsville was terrific. Kiwitahi was passed in 7.4 min (peak 54 mph) and Walton in 15 min 35 sec, but we dropped the tablet there! From Matamata we roared away again to average 47 mph uphill over the 12 miles to Tirau. From Hinerua to Okoroire the average speed was 56 mph.'

* Pulling out of Hamilton on No. 133 and suddenly crossing busy Victoria Street amid the stream of waiting city traffic, and then just as suddenly soaring over the Waikato River on the old high level lattice girder bridge, with the river far below the car windows.

* The unique brick water towers at Tirau, Putaruru and Ngatira. Apart from being brick, they were very attractive architecturally.

* Thoughts of the Roturua line and its tourist traffic inevitably lead to memories of the many excursion and tourist specials that ran over the years in steam days. Prior to the war two or three tourist specials were run from each cruise ship, all double headed by Ab engines east of Frankton. The last series of such trains were run between 1952 and 1956. Hauled by K engines, and providing the best accommodation available in 56 ft first-class cars, they made the run on a very fast 5 hr schedule. They represented the last high note in steam passenger service on the Rotorua line.

In 1927, long before the fame of New York's
Madison Avenue as an advertising place, the
Publicity Branch of the NZR concocted this
remarkable photo-montage of the Rotorua Express
on the Waikato Bridge at Hamilton with a Gipsy
Moth flying overhead, and a crowded paddle-wheel
steamer churning downstream below the train. The
steamer came from the Wanganui River.
Of course, the 'star' of the picture is the Rotorua
Express itself with its resplendent Ab engine still
fairly new, and the uniform set of fanlight windowed
mainline cars, except for the fifth which is a 'birdcage' type. The train looks assured and enduring
on the massive Victorian Era railway bridge, and
no one seriously thought in those times that the
aeroplane, as represented by the flimsy two-seater
overhead, would in a generation or so outdo the train
as an inter-city public carrier of passengers.

The Napier Express

The Napier Express had its distinctive journey highlights in the Manawatu Gorge, the Ruahine Ranges, and the many miles of curved and undulating track through the hilly sheep country of Hawkes Bay. It had its origins in the completion of the gorge line in 1891. Initially, the trip from Wellington to Napier was via the Wellington and Manawatu Railway to Longburn (opened in 1886), but in 1897 with the completion of the Wairarapa line through to the Woodville junction, the Napier Mail ran all the way over NZR metals via the Rimutakas, with connections to and from Palmerston North by way of the Gorge. This arrangement lasted until 1909 when the train was re-routed over the Manawatu line which had been taken over by the NZR in the previous year.

Palmerston North, Woodville junction, Dannevirke, Waipukurau, Hastings and Napier were the main stops identified with the run of the Napier Express, centres of public involvement, and sources of the route's economic sustenance. They were towns which had enveloped and absorbed the railway since pioneer times. I travelled to Napier on the Express (No. 612) in the spring of 1937. A lively Ab-hauled train of ten total, I recall it dashing past the streets of these towns into the busy stations with many waiting taxis, cars and vans, and well-filled station yards, so different from today's deserted scene. These glimpses were full of the mysterious fascination of places only known through the train window. Palmerston North and Hastings were both railway towns in the tradition of Christchurch and Ashburton in the South Island where the railway went right through the middle of town on the level with numerous street crossings. Beyond Palmerston North, at least five trains are recalled: the down express at Whakaronga, the 6.15 a.m. Napier-Palmerston North Mixed at Woodville, the 9.47 a.m. Palmerston North-Napier Mixed overtaken

A resplendent looking Napier Express (No. 612) leaving Wellington in 1938 with K engine No. 916 on the head end. The train is crossing over the Hutt Road preparatory to plunging into Tawa Tunnel No. 1, the first on the then newly opened Tawa Flat deviation. The K class engine and matching set of 50 ft centre-lavatory steel cars represent the ultimate development of the Napier Mail.

at Takapau, the 3.25 p.m. Waipukurau-Palmerston North Passenger (No. 931) at Clive.

These towns broke the run up into distinct segments: the Manawatu line shared with the Main Trunk and New Plymouth expresses to Palmerston North; the Manawatu Gorge to Woodville junction; the country of the upper Manawatu to Dannevirke with the Ruahines to the west; then a major hill section with deep ravines and lofty viaducts leading to the Takapau Plains and Waipukurau; more hills, and finally the Heretaunga plains and the twin towns of Hastings and Napier. The highest point on the line is a summit of over 1,000 ft on the Piri Piri side of Matamau (north of Dannevirke). The well-known viaducts encountered in this region, between Dannevirke and Takapau, were, (1) Mangatera (82 ft high) (2) Piri Piri (97 ft), (3) Matamau (99 ft), (4) Maketutu (85 ft), (5) Ormondville (129 ft) and (6) Kopua (95 ft). Important river crossings were the Tukituki near Waipukurau, the Waipawa at Waipawa, and the Ngaruroro and Tutaekuri rivers between Hastings and Napier. One of the more memorable moments of the journey was beyond Clive when the express burst into view of the sea near the Tutaikuri river bridge after a day's travel inland. Severe speed restrictions of as low as 20 mph were imposed on the viaducts, and there was a major restriction to 25 mph in the Manawatu Gorge over the six miles of more or less continuous curvature.

Notwithstanding these restrictions and the many miles of hill running, long stretches of easy track permitted the full 50 mph maximum, and in fact the Napier Express was marginally faster than the New Plymouth Express with an average speed between stops of 32.3 mph in 1939 in the up direction, compared with 30.8 mph for the up New Plymouth Express. The journey time was 7 hr 17 min, improved from 7 hr 31 min in 1925 (the year of the big speed up), and 9 hr 4 min in 1914. Perhaps, the most impressive feat of the Napier Express was over the Manawatu line in the war years when McGavin (of the *New Zealand Railway Observer*) recorded a huge train of eighteen cars weighing 475 tons and hauled by a single Ka, No. 949, running from Palmerston North to Paekakariki. By contrast, Ab-831 with a light pre-war load of seven was timed in 1939 at 58 mph, also on the Manawatu line.

Locomotives working on the Napier Express make a fascinating story. Prior to 1900, J class 2-6-0s were used. At about the turn of the century the Baldwin N Class Prairies of 1865 were brought up from the South Island and used in conjunction with M class 2-4-4 tank engines (converted from 0-6-0T). The latter were rather ineffectual engines, derisively called the 'Pullets' by engine men. Sometimes they were used in pairs on the Mail, and at other times in company with an N, when the duo would be referred to as a ''en and chicken'. Among the N's No. 27 with the Vauclain Compound cylinders was a very well-known engine on the Mail between 1901 and

The northbound Napier Mail running through the Square in Palmerston North about the year 1910, not long after the NZR took over the Wellington & Manawatu Line. The venerable old J class 2-6-0 displays a good head of steam for its important assignment, apparently not to be outdone by the Baldwin N's which were more often used.

1920. During the years 1891-1897 when the Mail ran over the Rimutakas, the connecting train from Palmerston North was hauled by Wa tank engines. Soon after the take-over of the Manawatu line, its two famous Baldwin Tenwheelers (4-6-0s), class Ud on the NZR, were used on the Napier Mail for three years. These 'high flyers' gave the train quite a bit of dash, and although no running records survived, it is more than likely that they would have used their big drivers to advantage when the occasion called for it. After this came the Standard Era, hailed by the introduction of the A class Pacifics (4-6-2s) around 1917-8 when the Ab's started taking over on the Main Trunk. Strangely enough, there is no history of A engines on the New Plymouth line, but they had a very good innings on the Napier Mail (later Express) until the early 1930s, when the ubiquitous Ab's took over. Ka and J classes infiltrated the postwar years of the express. During the war years, when long and heavy trains became the order of the day, the express was frequently double-headed by Ab's north of Palmerston North. A novel interlude in the 1930s was the occasional use of Bb 4-8-0s to take the express from Woodville Junction to Palmerston North through the gorge.

With regard to passenger stock, the Napier Express always had its share of the newest wooden Mainline cars from the Petone shops during the Standard Era, and for most of this period the train had a 'birdcage' car incorporated in its makeup. Soon after 1930 wooden Main Trunk cars, displaced by steel-panelled stock on that line, were transferred to the Napier Express service, where they ran until they in turn were displaced by a batch of steel-panel centre-lavatory Mainline cars built in 1935 specially for the Napier run. These cars formed the backbone of the train over most of its remaining years, and it is interesting that the Napier line was chosen ahead of the New Plymouth for the first steel panel stock on the Wellington provincial expresses. More than likely the keen road competition from Newman's buses had something to do with the decision.

There was an interesting history of postal cars on the Napier Mail; it was from these cars that the term mail train originated. They ran on the train right from its inception – from Napier to Palmerston North from 1891 to 1897, then from Wellington to Napier via the Wairarapa when the train ran over this route to 1909, and from then on via the Manawatu until the service was withdrawn in 1931. Pahiatua was the R.T.P.O. changeover point in the Wairarapa (the Mail trains crossed there), and Makotuku and Matamata were changeover points on the Napier to Palmerston North section at different times.

In the early 1920s, there was increasingly heavy road competition. The Napier Mail probably had more than its share of competition with two powerful concerns, the Hawkes Bay Motor

Opposite:
Another photo of the Napier Mail Connection taken in the early years of the century. The locale is a spectacular one at the eastern end of the Manawatu Gorge, and the engine is again a Wa class tank engine. The graceful old truss span taking the highway across the river was only recently demolished.

Below:
The southbound mail toiling up the Incline around the year 1907. Up front is the NZR's only Mallet-type locomotive, the controversial E-66 specially built in 1906 for the Incline.

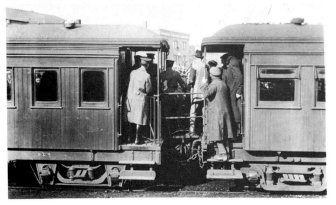

Farewelling volunteers at Dannevirke, a scene typical at railway stations all over New Zealand during the First World War years.

The first photo shows volunteers and wellwishers awaiting the arrival of a troop train. There is even a band ready for the occasion. Prominent in the background is the highly ornate colonial-style railway hotel, an indispensable adjunct to any important station.

In the second photo the special has arrived in charge of an A class compound, seen just to the right of the gothic-looking signal cabin. The flat roof, small window cars are bogie rebuilds of colonial 4-wheelers. Seating will be of the longitudinal bench type.

The third photo shows some of the departing passengers crowding the carriage platforms and gangway to get a last view of it all. There is special interest in the graphic comparison it provides of the progress in carriage design between the first arch roof design of the 1890s (left) and the second series of mainline cars of about 1910 (right). Note the lighter bogie of the earlier car with its single inside equaliser bar and two slender bolster springs as compared with the much more solid bogie of 1910 with its twin equaliser bars and four bolster springs. Note also the bigger windows and fanlights on the later car. The evolutionary trends are very apparent, but both are very much NZR-style cars in design and construction.

World War I called for the biggest sustained mass movement of people by the NZR up to that time. Out of a population of 1,000,000, 120,000 served in the forces with 100,000 going overseas. 18,500 died and 50,000 were wounded. This tremendous military effort required countless special trains; the dependence on the railway at that time was absolute.

World War I was something of a watershed for the NZR. By then it was well embarked upon policies that would enable it to be well up with the great standard era of railways of the 1920s and 1930s. The A class engine and standard mainline car seen at Dannevirke were rolling stock developments which would lead the NZR into the new post war era. The famous Ab express engine was designed and introduced during the World War I period. At the same time the end of the war was to see the end of old cars as seen in photo two and the numerous classes of obsolete engines like them.

Company and the Aard Company both running rival services. Known as service cars, the motors (in the case of the Hawkes Bay Motor Company) largely comprised nine-seater Cadillacs. However, to some extent there was collaboration between rail and road beyond Napier to Wairoa and Gisborne in that rail passengers had to complete their journeys to those places by road in the long period before the line was extended. But there was ruinous cut-throat competition for the road traffic as three companies, the Hawkes Bay Motor Company, Whitfield's, and the Duco Company, all fought it out for the business. The Duco Company was one of owner drivers, and the NZR's problem with motor competition was seen from the fact that it was possible to purchase a Studebaker or a Hudson for £50 deposit from eager salesmen, and start up in the passenger transport business.

This led to remarkable scenes at the Napier railway station on the arrival of the Mail from Wellington at 5 p.m. Passenger buses of the three companies would be waiting outside, while drivers and agents for the companies moved up and down the station platform. The arrival of the train heralded pandemonium as arriving passengers were rushed. As Len Anderson in his book *Coaches North* says: 'No tourist in Cairo besieged by the gali-gali men was under greater pressure than the unassuming New Zealander stepping off the train on to the Napier railway station platform. Passengers' luggage labels would be examined by half a dozen strangers; they would be told vehicles were waiting, and hustled into one of the line-up of motor cars outside the station entrance.' Allied with all this turmoil were situations where, in the case of passengers with checked luggage, one company would finish up with the luggage and another with the passenger, a tricky confrontation in which a good deal of diplomacy was needed. This state of affairs, which had parallels in other parts of New Zealand at the time, must have raised doubts in many minds as to the real virtues of 'laissez-faire' economics, and when a few years later a system of licensing of transport operators was introduced, many people approved of it.

Previous page:
The Napier Mail crossing
the Ormondville Viaduct.

Bob Stott, railway author and journalist of Wellington, has first-hand memories of the Napier Express from childhood days at Waipukurau in the 1940s.

He recalls with perception and nostalgia 'a rather war-worn railway, which nonetheless was still of vital importance to the communities it served. . . There were always dozens of people on the platform even in a town of less than 3,000. It was a bit of a performance. The tablet bells rang out, and the refreshment room staff alerted. The signals would come off, and then there would be a wait. You could not see up or down the line owing to the curves at each end of the yard. Then the tablet porter would appear with a tablet in a sling — there was no exchanger as there was always a lot of passenger traffic, and apart from trains stopping in any case, an ex-

When, sometime about 1911-1912, an unknown photographer set up his plate camera beside the Mangatera Viaduct, about 1½ miles north of Dannevirke and just south of the Piri Piri Summit to take a picture of the Down Napier Mail, it is probable that he little dreamed that sixty years later it would be regarded as something of a masterpiece of its kind. Even in the recent period of specialisation in train photography, a better combination of composition, scenic location, train interest and clarity of detail would be hard to find. The engine which adds its own lustre to the occasion is one of the famous pair of tall-drivered Baldwin Tenwheelers, the 'high flyers' of the former Wellington & Manawatu Railway Co.

changer could clobber the people. Then the train would appear, always with a Ka, seemingly coming in slowly, but really going at quite a belt as it passed under the station verandah. The train would stop when signalled right opposite the invariably quite large pile of van work on the platform, and the passengers would rush off to the refreshment rooms. Hardly had the train stopped than the engine would be uncoupled and run off up the yard for water. Then there would be a pause for the munching, the filling, the van work, and so on, until the tender tank lid would slam shut and the engine would back down on to the train again. The station bell would ring a warning, the guard would blow his whistle and wave his green flag, there would be a shrill blast from the engine whistle, and away would go the train. There were always good passenger loads, the vans were full of roadside work, and the trains always seemed more or less on time, at least to within five or ten minutes at the outside.'

Set out below is a summary of the 1939 timetable for the Napier Express, showing its connections with the Wairarapa Mail and the New Plymouth Express in the southbound direction:

TIMETABLE WELLINGTON-NAPIER EXPRESS SERVICE 1939

HASL	M	Stations	No. 612 Exp. Daily		No. 913 Exp. Daily	
—	—	Wellington	dep	9.40 a.m.	arr	4.00 p.m.
100	87	Palmerston N (R)	arr	12.14 p.m.	dep	1.08 p.m.
			dep	12.25 p.m.	arr	12.50 p.m. (c)
261	105	Woodville Jc (R)	arr	1.16 p.m.	dep	12.40 p.m.
			dep	1.31 p.m.	arr	11.55 a.m. (a)
680	121	Dannevirke	dep	2.10 p.m.	dep	11.27 a.m.
435	156	Waipukurau (R)	dep	3.30 p.m.	dep	9.58 a.m.
38	187	Hastings	dep	4.37 p.m.	dep	8.57 a.m.
10	199	Napier	arr	4.57 p.m.	dep	8.28 a.m.

(a) change for Wairarapa line

(c) connects with New Plymouth Express dep Palmerston North 1.00 p.m.

Nos. 612 and 913 crossed at Whakarongo flag station four miles east of Palmerston North.

(R = refreshment station).

Not the 'Golden Age' of the steam train by any means, but the railway did count for something. Our local station even had its own engine, an A or Aa, which would work a daily goods down the line, and that train was really important. There was work at most stations, and I can recall goods trains with the van so full that a roadsider would be added. Tin cans of movie film, racing pigeons, boxes of wet fish, bicycles, dogs, papers and magazines, cases of fruit, always sacks of mail and wicker hampers of fragile parcels, as well anonymous bits and pieces by the dozen.

That was my railway. My father worked on it, and as a result I spent a good slice of my school holidays on it. It was an intimate railway, in close relationship to the community, and yet at the same time a community in itself.'

The old Napier Mail rounding Rocky Point, five miles out of Wellington, early one morning in 1901, during the years that the train ran via the Wairarapa. This must be one of the most remarkable collections of locomotives and rolling stock ever seen on any mail train in New Zealand. It could be a real life creation from the railway phantasy world of Emmett's cartoons in Punch, or from the drawings of that master of the quaint and eccentric, W. Heath Robinson. Leading this fascinating procession, are two very diverse tank engines, an American (Baldwin) Wb class 2-6-2 engine of 1898, and separated by a runner wagon, an English-built (Avonside Engine Co.) S class 0-6-4 Fairlie's Patent of 1880.

Ka-952 on the Gisborne-Wellington Express at Dannevirke, around 1950. A melancholy aspect of the scene is the drastic thinning of the platform crowds. Associated with this is the incongruity of the huge Ka engine, the last work in NZR steam technology, with only four cars and a van to handle.

The Gisborne Express

*I*naugurated on 7 September 1942 on completion of the new line, the Gisborne Express service became the longest provincial run in New Zealand (328 miles). Timetabling presented the NZR with some awkward problems, especially in the southbound direction. With the provision of the through express in each direction the southbound departure from Napier and Hastings would have been too late to suit most of the lucrative business from these two centres. The early morning departure of the Napier Express for Wellington had been an institution for generations, and to substitute an afternoon departure with a very late evening arrival in Wellington would have caused an outcry. Apart from this, Newmans were well established as aggressive road competitors, and there was reason to fear the loss of further business to the highway.

So at first there was a through express only in the northbound direction. This was simply an extension of the former Napier Express (No. 612) through to Gisborne, leaving Wellington at the same time of 9.40 a.m. and arriving Gisborne 11.05 p.m. It was possible to travel from Gisborne to Wellington on Tuesdays and Thursdays, but this was by a series of connecting trains taking from 10.05 a.m. to 11.40 p.m. to complete the journey. A through southbound express, No. 931, was introduced on 10 January 1944, leaving Gisborne at 8.55 a.m. and arriving in Wellington at 10.10 p.m. This train lasted only three weeks when it was cancelled on account of the coal shortage. It was restored to three times per week on 7 September 1944, and with its northbound running mate remained on this frequency for the rest of its career except for holiday times. As road and air competition increased this restricted schedule was a serious handicap in competing for what was only a relatively moderate amount of through travel from Gisborne to Wellington.

13 September, 1942: Much of the old-time feeling of a great public occasion was there when 10,000 Gisbornites turned up to see the first passenger train leave Gisborne for Napier, double-headed by two Ab engines. It was an occasion for high hopes, even though the prospect of a first passenger train from Gisborne to Auckland had by then become an empty dream.

A few miles south of Poverty Bay a 1957 Easter-time Gisborne-Wellington Express (G-31) in a scenic setting in the Maraetaha Valley. The engines are Ab's 736 and 738. At this stage express trains had shrunk to holiday times only.

A major improvement in the timetable took place in May 1948. No. 612 left Wellington twenty-eight minutes earlier at 9.12 a.m. and arrived at Gisborne 1 h 10 min earlier at 9.55 p.m. There was a better improvement to the southbound No. 931 which left Gisborne at 7.10 a.m. and arrived in Wellington nearly three hours earlier at 7.15 p.m. in time to connect with the South Island ferry service.

The Gisborne Express left Wellington with some impressive formations during wartime, such as No. 612 leaving Wellington behind Ed-108 with a fifteen or sixteen total. The cars were a more or less random assortment of some of the 50 ft steel mainline cars originally built for the Napier Express in 1935, and wooden mainline cars of various series.

About ten of the cars would have come off at Napier. After the 1944 coal cuts, second-class passengers were carried in old Main Trunk cars converted to seat fifty-one people, but before Easter 1945 the pre-war Napier Express cars were restored to the service. For the first accelerated service on 3 May 1948, No. 931 was reported as being made up of the usual eleven vehicles, but the three seconds in the Gisborne section on this occasion were of the older mainline type. Ab-740 handled the train on the Gisborne-Napier section and Ka-934 from Napier to Paekakariki.

Improvements to equipment continued, and in August 1949 the Gisborne section of Nos. 612 and 931 included two ex-ambulance cars (Nos. 1978 and 1986) reconverted to standard 56 ft seconds, and two 56 ft seconds (Nos. 1905 and 1928) refurbished with new reclining seats to seat thirty-five and reclassified first-class. These cars were to have been the prototypes of a wholesale and very desirable upgrading of 56 ft seconds generally, but the plan was dropped and the converted cars remained in use as firsts. The Gisborne section of Nos. 612 and 931 was now fully vestibuled.

In 1950 No. 612 was recorded as leaving Wellington with the following make-up: Ed-105, cars 1840, 1831, 1837, 1978, 1986, 1970, 1905, vans F-597 and Z-397. The first three cars made up the Napier section and comprised two seconds and one first of the 1935-6 Napier Express cars. At this stage the Gisborne Express achieved its highest standard of equipment. However, erosion of traffic and the impending replacement of provincial expresses by railcars caused the NZR to lose interest, and before long the 56 ft firsts were replaced by two ex-Main Trunk 50 ft steel firsts of the early 1930s.

The Gisborne Express made its last run in regular service in 1955, when it was replaced by articulated railcars. Its relatively short life of thirteen years was not enough for it to have built up the sort of tradition the Napier and New Plymouth Expresses did. Apart from the few war years, it operated in an era when the steam passenger train was on the decline.

The Auckland-New Plymouth Night Expresses were the least photographed and the most short-lived of all New Zealand's express trains. This is train No. 247/518 leaving Stratford Junction at 6.06 a.m. one early morning in 1940, for the last lap of the run to New Plymouth. There was a connecting train at Stratford for Hawera.

The Auckland-New Plymouth Night Expresses

Night expresses between Auckland and New Plymouth were inaugurated with the opening of the Stratford Line in September 1933, and remained the main form of passenger service until replaced by railcars in November 1956. The 89-mile Stratford Line provided the essential link between Okahukura Junction on the Main Trunk and Stratford in Taranaki. It took thirty-two years to build, but ran through much very rugged bush country, especially at the northern end. There were no fewer than twenty-four tunnels and many stretches of gradient at between 1 in 50 and 1 in 60 as the line traversed successions of ridges. Okahukura Junction was seven miles north of Taumaranui, creating something of a handicap for expresses making the Taumarunui stop by increasing the overall Auckland-New Plymouth journey by fourteen miles to a total of 300 miles.

The inaugural night express from Auckland left on 3 September 1933, and comprised one second-class car, one first-class, a composition sleeping car, and a guard's van. It ran to Taumarunui attached to the Auckland-Wellington Limited which then departed at 7.00 p.m. There, the New Plymouth portion was detached, and with an Ab engine in charge, it ran via the new line to New Plymouth, where it arrived at 6.06 a.m. next day. In the reverse direction, the express departed New Plymouth at 7.10 p.m. and at Taumaranui was attached to the Wellington-Auckland Express, arriving at Auckland at 7.10 next morning. The service was operated three days per week in each direction, an arrangement that lasted for several years. At holiday times, a separate express would run from Auckland and travel direct down the Stratford Line from Ohahukura. A special from Taumarunui would connect with it there to cater for passengers from that station. There was a similar arrangement in the reverse direction.

In 1940 a completely separate tri-weekly through-service was introduced with Nos. 247 and 518 leaving Auckland at 7.50 p.m. every Sunday, Tuesday and Thursday, and Nos. 430 and 531 which left New Plymouth on Mondays, Wednesdays and Fridays at 7.08 p.m. and arrived in Auckland at 6.30 next morning. The sleeping car facilities disappeared with the war and the coal-saving cuts of December 1944. Towards the end of the war, conditions had worsened, and by 1950 the service had diminished to two expresses each way per week.

TIMETABLE AUCKLAND-NEW PLYMOUTH NIGHT EXPRESS 1943				
HASL	*M*	*Stations*	*Train No. 247* *Sun Tu Thur*	*Train No. 430* *Tu Thur Sat*
9	—	Auckland	dep 7.50 p.m.	arr 6.30 a.m.
123	85	Frankton Jc (R)	arr 10.16 p.m. dep 10.26 p.m.	dep 4.00 a.m. arr 3.49 a.m.
561	174	Taumarunui (R)	arr 1.40 a.m.	dep 12.40 a.m.
			Train No. 518 *Mon Wed Fri* dep 1.50 a.m.	*Train No. 531* *Mon Wed Fri* arr 12.22 a.m.
1011	271	Stratford Jc	dep 6.06 a.m.	dep 8.30 a.m.
14	300	New Plymouth	arr 7.19 a.m.	dep 7.08 p.m.

I had some trips on these trains in 1950 and 1951, when the usual make-up was two 56 ft first-class cars, three 56 ft seconds, and a van at each end. Auckland Station then presented a lively scene with the Limited at Platform 2 and the New Plymouth at Platform 1. The engines were usually J-class, and we finished up with J's at New Plymouth. Patronage was quite reasonable on all trips. The extra doubling-up of the seven miles from Okahukura Junction to Taumarunui and the reversing of the seats there, was a curious feature of the trip, although many passengers would have dozed through it.

One of my journeys was the coldest I ever remember anywhere. The Stratford Line was no place for the steam heating to play up during the wintertime. I recall a stop at a station named Matiere, surely on this occasion one of the coldest and most desolate outposts on the NZR. Even the humble tablet stations on the Main Trunk always seemed to have a reassuring air of life and warmth about them, but this place with its eerie, murky half light and unearthly quiet seemed more like a setting for the well known 'Ghost Train' of theatre fame. The night was pitch black, and there was not a single light to be seen beyond the station. At one stage I could hear the echoing and spasmodic footsteps of what was probably the porter-in-charge. Everything was quiet in the dark carriage; not even the 'glug-glug' of a steam valve. We stayed there for quite a long time, for reasons which remain a mystery. Certainly no train arrived from the opposite direction to make a crossing. There seemed to be an air of unreality about it, so far as a ride on an express train was concerned.

The Auckland-New Plymouth Night Expresses, and their nocturnal runs, may not be as well remembered as some other provincial express trains. They had a relatively short life span of twenty-three years. In latter years, when the main highway was sealed, competing buses had the advantage of a road distance of 241 miles compared to 300 for the train. The buses had the advantage, too, in that they offered daylight travel through what was a very scenic countryside. When the aeroplane appeared on the scene, competition was intensified. Even as far back as the 1950s the old N.A.C. Dakotas were doing the run in under an hour. However, the express run to New Plymouth was a very interesting experience in train travel, and one with its own particular character. And the Auckland-New Plymouth Expresses added another dimension to the railway passenger scene at a time when there were four provincial expresses operating out of Auckland as well as the two Main Trunk expresses.

Train No. 247/518, the overnight express from Auckland via the Stratford line, arrives at New Plymouth on a sunny morning in early 1951 with a train-load of sleepy-eyed passengers aboard. The engine is Jb-1229 and the cars are all 56 ft stock (two first-class and three seconds).

The New Plymouth Express

While there were certain basic similarities between the New Plymouth and Napier expresses over the years, the west and east coast routes were rather different in character. Probably the New Plymouth line possessed more facets of interest. Most impressive and distinctive was the 50-mile run from Hawera to New Plymouth under the shadow of Mt Egmont; it might have been more appropriate to call it 'The Egmont Express', just as in Japan there is a 'Fujiyama Express'. The New Plymouth run was considerably longer than the Napier, 251 miles as against 190 miles. In fact, it was the longest provincial run in New Zealand prior to the opening of the Gisborne line in 1942. Also, there was a pleasing diversity in the five junctions beyond Palmerston North: Marton (for the Main Trunk), Aramoho (for Wanganui), Te Roti (for Opunake), Stratford (for Okahukura), and Lepperton (for Waitara).

The New Plymouth Express was the longest established of the NZR provincial services. Through rail service between Wellington and New Plymouth became available in December 1886 via the newly completed Wellington and Manawatu Railway to Longburn and the NZR from thereon. The service departed from Thorndon at 7 a.m. on Tuesdays and Fridays and took 15 hours including meal stops at Halcombe and Patea. Connections were made at New Plymouth with the overnight steamer service to Onehunga for Auckland. (A special boat train ran from the Onehunga wharf to Auckland). In 1901 the service became a daily one with a 7.25 a.m. departure and a journey of 12 hr 50 min and remained on a daily basis throughout most of the train's existence until the coal shortage cuts in 1944. The Onehunga steamer connections disappeared with the inauguration of the Main Trunk express in 1909. To provide the faster schedule, through trains avoiding the transfer at Palmerston North were arranged with the co-operation of the

Opposite:
The scene at New Plymouth station soon after the arrival of a long excursion train from Wanganui on a summer Sunday morning in the late 1930s. The siding on the left was provided for passenger trains to and from the port to meet the steamers from Auckland in the days before the opening of the Main Trunk. The one on the right is a general service siding: on this occasion it is accomodating 'Way & Works' vehicles.

Wellington & Manawatu Company. The government trains were worked right through on four days per week, and the Wellington & Manawatu trains on the other two days. The New Plymouth Mail as it was known at the time became a wholly NZR operation when the Wellington & Manawatu Company was taken over by the government in 1908.

An advanced feature of the New Plymouth Mail trains in the early 1900s was the provision of dining cars. Three cars were built by the NZR for the run in 1901-2, and it is interesting to note that this train was the second, after the Christchurch-Dunedin Express, to be so equipped. These cars were 44 ft long, and had gas cooking facilities. However, the Wellington & Manawatu Company stole the thunder of the NZR in 1904 by introducing a 52 ft dining car, the largest running in New Zealand. This car was equipped with electric lighting, had a 26 ft long dining saloon, and a very roomy kitchen. It would have worked through to New Plymouth with the Manawatu Company's train set. The dining cars were withdrawn in 1917. Another interesting vehicle on these trains at this time was the standard type of wooden postal van, marshalled next to the engine. Passenger cars generally comprised the first series of wooden mainline cars on the NZR trains, while the Manawatu trains were made up with that company's distinctive and handsome clerestory roof American cars.

Over the first two decades of the present century, the New Plymouth Mail was notable for the remarkable variety of motive power it employed. In the remaining Manawatu Company years after the turn of the century the Company's Baldwin Oc class 2-8-0s and Bc 2-8-2s took the Mail out of Wellington over the hills to Paekakariki where the high-drivered Ud class ten-wheelers took over for the run along the coastal plain to Longburn, the connecting point with the NZR. Here, the Ud would be replaced by Palmerston North based Wa 2-6-2 and Wf 2-6-4 tank engines of the NZR, as well as Wanganui based Wb 2-6-2 tank engines further on. But most astonishing were the E class 0-4-0/0-4-0 Fairlie engines stationed at New Plymouth for work on the Mail. Even further novelty was added when in the early 1900s some 'spruced up' M class 2-4-4 tank engines were sent to New Plymouth to assist in the working of the Mail.

For a couple of years after the NZR took over the Wellington & Manawatu Railway Company the Ud's ran right through from Paekakariri to Marton, sometimes with a Wa or a Wf helper from Palmerston North. By then, the new A class compounds were steadily taking over all express workings on the Manawatu Line, but curiously enough the Wf's and other tank engines continued to play a big part in the haulage of the Mail right through until the Ab era in the 1920s. There was no intervening use of the A's or Q's as elsewhere. Bridge standards probably had something to do with it, but the sight of two spanking new Wf's with their huge brass steam domes dazzling

In the last years of the Wellington & Manawatu Railway Company: the New Plymouth Mail leaves Thorndon on New Year's Day 1907 hauled by one of the Company's improved Prairie (2-6-2) type Baldwins driven by Vauclain Compound propulsion. Thick steam exhaust at the rear of the train points to a banking engine pushing hard, and it is almost certain to be the redoubtable Jumbo, the 2-8-4 Baldwin tank engine specially built for the job of assisting trains out of Thorndon. On the lower left of the Manawatu line's embankment can be seen the NZR line to the Hutt and the Wairarapa, flexing around the shoreline of the harbour. This was the route used at the time by the Napier Mail. The Hutt Road in the foreground with a lone pedestrian strolling down the centre makes a very striking contrast to today's motoways.

Throughout the steam passenger train era, and wherever the trains ran, people took time off to watch them go by. Here in Levin sometime about 1905, a group of locals stop to watch Manawatu Company's new Baldwin Prairie-type engine work a formidable 19 total New Plymouth Express out of town. The front three cars are NZR stock, a 1900 American compartment car, a Petone 'birdcage' car of 1896-7, and an early arch roof type of 1897. The rest of the train is entirely Wellington & Manawatu, and with the Baldwin engine and American style clerestory roof cars was very similar to most American trains of the day.

Nothing could be more typical of express train operation out of Wellington in the mid-1930s than this photo of the New Plymouth Express double-headed with Ab engines fighting the grades between Khandallah and Johnsonville on the old Manawatu Company's mainline out of the capital. This photo had the distinction of being reproduced in the popular part work 'Railway Wonders of the World' of 1935, and enthusiasts of the day thought it was very aptly chosen. Tawny hills, sharp reverse curves, Ab engines, standard wooden mainline cars: all were so representative of the New Zealand railway scene.

in the sun as they left Palmerston with the Mail was a memorable one.

Interesting engine workings on the Mail were recalled by Mr W.W. Stewart; during an up trip in 1918 a Bb 4-8-0 hauled the Mail from Marton to Aramoho, a Ww 4-6-4 tank banked by a Wg 4-6-4 tank did the job from there to Hawera, and thenceforth a Wf 2-6-4 tank to New Plymouth.

Throughout the so-called Standard Era from 1920 to 1940 the Express, as it became later was always made up with carriages from the latest series of wooden mainline cars. In 1935 it was made up with a distinctive set of the fourth and last series of wooden mainline cars only just built, and distinguished from the earlier series by a single steel fascia, angle iron trusses, and roller bearing bogies. However, during wartime this set was dispersed, and the express became a rather motley mixture of assorted cars until it was re-equipped in 1948.

In the 1920s typical loadings comprised nine to ten cars and a van, but during the Depression of the early 1930s the loading was as light as six. As times improved after 1935 the loadings increased, to about eight and nine at the beginning of the war. Throughout the Standard Era the Express was hauled by Ab engines, with assisting Wab's out of Wellington to Paekakariki and Wf's over the notorious Fordell Bank between Marton and Aramoho. Double heading was standard practice during holiday times and other periods of heavy loading.

At this time the general practice was for a New Plymouth Ab engine and crew to run the down Express (No. 507) as far as Aramoho, uncouple, then run into Wanganui with the Branch connection ('The Ferry' as it was called). The Wanganui Ab which brought the Ferry (plus any through Wanganui-Wellington cars) into the junction would meantime couple on to No. 507 and the express would continue on to Marton.

Before long the New Plymouth Ab would return to Aramoho with the Ferry to connect with No. 610, (the up express, which it would work on to New Plymouth). The Wanganui Ab off No. 610 (plus any Wellington-Wanganui through cars) would then run into Wanganui with the Ferry. The New Plymouth engine crew would have quite a long day from 7.45 a.m. to 8.00 p.m.

Towards the end of the 1930s the K and later Ka engines handled the workings of Nos. 507 and 610, like the other expresses, over the Manawatu Line to Palmerston North and Marton according to loadings and engine availability. During wartime the big 4-8-4s rolled some very heavy loads single-handed over this stretch. A typical example recorded in the *New Zealand Railway Observer* in 1944 related how Ka-961 hauled a seventeen-car version of No. 610 with a gross load of 415 tons at a speed of 60 mph through Levin, and ran from there to Makerau, a distance of 13.6 miles at an average of 51.8 mph.

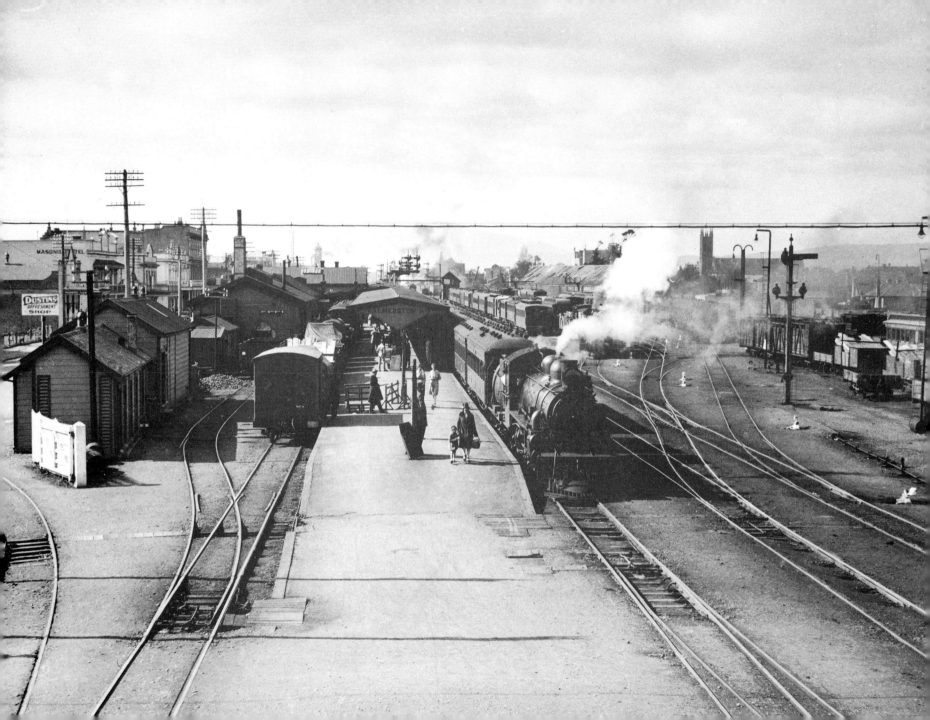

Late one sunny afternoon, sometime, in the mid 1920s, a discerning photographer took this view of the down New Plymouth Express making its daily routine stop at Palmerston North. These were good times for the passenger train — perhaps the best ever. Passenger service was still intact on all the branch lines in both first and second-class accommodation, even though only two to three days per week on some of the more remote ones. It was only towards the end of the 1920s that these services began to disappear under the onslaught of bus competition. On the trunk and provincial lines a uniformly modern standard of passenger accommodation had been evolved with the introduction of hundreds of up-to-date wooden carriages which had been built in the past decade and which were still coming off the assembly lines at Newmarket and Addington. The cluttered up yards were on a very comprehensible scale; today's yards are remote and empty by comparison. In those days when even comparatively small merchants sported their own sidings, if only to dispatch and receive an odd wagon every now and again, interesting little spur lines sprouted out in all directions from the station yards, like the one curving away in the left foreground and protected by the clearly seen derailing switch. The house siding of the station itself can also be seen in the foreground holding an La wagon. Stores for the station were shunted in here, the main item being the coal for winter fires, and to stoke the footwarmer boilers housed in the outbuilding with the tall chimney.

Regular passenger service between Wanganui and Aramoho junction ceased in 1959, when the venerable old station assumed the forlorn faceless look that goes with 'freight only' operation, and became a backwater. Things were vastly different in 1940 when this photo of excursion trains at Wanganui was taken. As a scene of railway and attendant human activity it is very impressive. A formidable smoky streamlined Ka is double-heading with an Ab on the train loading up at the platform, while double-heading Ab's in the loop wait with a following train. Enginemen and other railwaymen seem to be enjoying the brief prelude to the action which is soon to follow.

After World War II, there was a gradual infiltration of the big engines into Taranaki, first the K's and Ka's, then the ubiquitous Ja's. At first the 4-8-4's ran in two segments: Palmerston North-Wanganui, and Wanganui-New Plymouth, with the same arrangements for working 'The Ferry' as described earlier. Later still, the 4-8-4s ran right through from New Plymouth to Palmerston North with the one crew, who would stay for the night and return home next day. The last regular steam-hauled New Plymouth Express was handled by Ja-1289. As might be expected, that inimitable Wanganui institution 'The Ferry', gave way to a dull bus service.

In August 1945 a new 56-ft first-class car was added and by 1948 the train was fully equipped with a set of 56-ft cars, and a 56-ft van. The first-class cars had compartments and a hostess service. A special through car for Wanganui was also provided for the first time, this being a 50-ft steel 'mainline' type, this car being detached and added at Aramoho on the northbound and southbound runs respectively. This was certainly a brave attempt to recapture past glories of the early 1900s, and the NZR deserved all credit for trying so hard in an age much less favourable to successful passenger train operation.

The overall journey time of the then Mail was further reduced over the years. In 1924 it was 11 hrs, and in 1939 was down to 9½ hrs in each direction. After the opening of the Turakina deviation in December 1947 it was reduced to 9¼ hrs after some rather longer wartime schedules.

TIMETABLE - NEW PLYMOUTH EXPRESS SERVICE - 1939

HASL	M	Stations	No. 610 Express Daily		No. 507 Express Daily	
8'	—	Wellington	dep	10.15 am	arr	5.55 pm
100'	87	Palmerston N (R)	dep	1.00 pm (X 913)	dep	3.16 pm
462'	116	Marton Jc (R)	arr	2.10 pm (X 507)	dep	2.07 pm
			dep	2.23 pm	arr	1.44 pm (X 610)
30'	147	Aramoho Jc (R) *	dep	3.45 pm	dep	12.27 pm
11'	185	Patea (R)	dep	5.16 pm	dep	10.51 am
344'	203	Hawera (R)	dep	6.20 pm	dep	10.14 am
1011'	221	Stratford Jc (R)	dep	6.48 pm	dep	9.37 am
14'	251	New Plymouth	arr	7.48 pm	dep	8.25 am

* Aramoho Jc: change for Wanganui
(R = refreshment station)

The Wairarapa Mail

The Wairarapa Mail on the 115-mile Wellington-Woodville run was, over the last decades of steam, the principal steam passenger service over the Rimutaka Ranges to Masterton and the other towns and communities of the Wairarapa plains and the Mangatainoka valley beyond. At Woodville, it provided Wairarapa passengers with connections for Napier and Palmerston North. In fact, the cars of the Mail worked through to the latter place as part of a mixed train. The Napier connections were with the Napier Expresses.

Few provincial passenger trains possessed such a distinctive character as the Wairarapa Mail. During the trip over the Rimutakas it traversed the famous Incline, based on the rare Fell system of centre rail traction, an operation which attracted world-wide interest. In the short run from Wellington to Masterton no fewer than three different engines were used, and these were of exceptional variety: modest Ww tank engines out of Wellington, the only aspiration of this class to provincial service; the quaint little 0-4-2 Fell engines, nearly as old as the NZR itself; and the Addington A's used in the Wairarapa. At holiday times as many as eight engines could be needed to get the Mail to Masterton. Only the West Coast Mail in the South Island could claim anything like such a variety of power.

Complete with its set of the earlier mainline-type of wooden cars — many remaining gaslit well into the 1930s and even later — the Mail remained an authentic specimen of the World War I era. The only change of any consequence was the appearance of Ab's on both sides of the Hill after World War II.

The origins of the Wairarapa Mail are unusual. Prior to 1897 the only rail route from Wellington to Napier was via the privately owned Wellington and Manawatu railway, with a change of

Wholly Smoke!!
This was the very apt caption of this famous NZR publicity photo when it was published in an overseas trade journal. Admirably capturing a fantastic display of loco-motive effort, it portrays the 1935 Royal Train of the Duke of Gloucester struggling up the Rimutaka Incline out of Cross Creek with five H class Fell engines supplying the tractive effort. In the middle background in the Cross Creek yard can be seen the two A class Pacifics which handled the train through the Wairarapa.

Leaving a flattened trail of exhaust to mark its going, Ww-569 hustles the northbound Wairarapa Mail around the shores of Wellington Harbour in what appears to be a major effort on the part of the modest-sized and ageing tank engine. This was the way the Mail looked in 1939. The sense of time and place is enhanced by the American-style signals of the automatic upper quadrant semaphore type which stand like sentinels on each side of the Mail. Apart from a minor installation between Arthur's Pass and Otira, these signals, installed in the mid-1920s, were an exclusive feature on the Wellington-Upper Hutt line. They were more or less standard practice on American mainlines, and, being operated by the trains themselves, were an early example of automation originating in the railway field.

train at Palmerston North. On completion of the Wellington-Woodville line in 1897 (the line to Masterton was opened in 1880), the NZR was able to assert its independence of the Wellington and Manawatu Railway by instituting a Napier Mail, running via the Wairarapa line. The train operated over the Rimutakas for twelve years until 1909, by which time the NZR had absorbed the Wellington and Manawatu railway and was able to switch the Napier Mail over to the much easier Manawatu route. The Wellington-Woodville remnant of the erstwhile Napier Mail became the Wairarapa Mail. Another interesting by-product of the takeover was the allocation of that line's high-drivered Baldwin Ud engines for use on the Wairarapa Mail.

The Wairarapa Mail was uniquely identified with the old Lambton Station. The directions were familiar: 'Thorndon for the Main Trunk, Napier and New Plymouth, Lambton for the Wairarapa'. The Mail was the mainline operation out of Lambton amid the host of Hutt Valley suburban trains. Among the author's earliest recollections of North Island trains was a trip to Masterton on the Mail in January 1930 to visit an uncle who was stationmaster there. We had crossed from Lyttelton on the old *Maori*, and it was an easy walk from the ship to Lambton where we did not have to wait long before the Mail was shunted in amidst the busy rush hour comings and goings of suburban trains. The Mail had to be handled smartly at Lambton. Although not differing greatly from many of the suburban trains, the uniform set of mainline cars with 'Palmerston North' destination boards up, plus the waiting passengers with their luggage, indicated that this was more than just another suburban operation. It was towards the end of the Lambton era: before long the historic old station was to be swallowed up in the present Wellington terminal.

When the new terminal was opened in 1937, all mainline trains were at last able to leave from the one station, and the Wairarapa Mail took its place with the others. However, the ageing Mail did not fit in as well as at Lambton. The magnificence of the new surroundings and the increasing proportion of new motive power and passenger cars on other important trains all served to make the Mail look more like a train from yesterday. It was still cherished by those who remained faithful to the traditional method of travel over the Rimutakas and railway amateurs who liked the standard era of the NZR, but time was running out.

The Wairarapa railcars introduced in 1936 had won considerable popularity as an up-to-date and much faster means of rail travel. Wartime conditions brought a revival in the fortunes of the train, which served the important Trentham Military Camp. Then came the drastic coal shortages of 1944 reducing the Mail to three services per week, a blow from which it never recovered. Four years later, it gave up the ghost, and the railcars took over all Wairarapa passenger services

Ww's 681 and 731 make a very brave showing as they burst out of a tunnel and cross the Mangaroa River on a slender trestle with the Wairarapa Mail sometime in the year 1939. No scene could have more of the hallmark of the NZR than this one of the stately homebuilt tank engines and the pioneer style bridge of which there were hundreds in use at one time.

except during holiday periods. It is an ironic postscript that when the long-promised tunnel was opened in 1955, the Mail had been gone for seven years. Perhaps, it was not altogether inappropriate that the Mail did not survive the Incline with which it had been so closely associated for so long in the popular imagination.

Over the years there was little change in the timetable of the Mail which ran on Monday to Saturday, except for the last few years when it was affected by coal shortage cuts. The 1939 timetable was typical.

The 5 h 32 min northbound and 5 h 31 min southbound for the sixty-six miles to Masterton reflected the barrier of the Incline. To negotiate its three miles took approximately forty minutes, but the complicated shunting at both ends meant that nearly a whole hour was consumed between the Summit and Cross Creek.

Summit, Labour Day 1943. The southbound Wairarapa Mail left Cross Creek at 4.17 p.m. and has surmounted the Incline. Now its three Fell engines have been cut out to return to Cross Creek, and a bunker-first Ww engine has taken its place at the head of the 8 total train, ready to leave for Wellington at 4.59 p.m. Stormy weather and a bleak landscape give a sombre mood to the scene.

However there was much to capture the attention of those who liked railways: the unusual yard layout designed to facilitate the marshalling of trains for the run down the Incline (and vice versa) and the actual marshalling operations themselves were unique in New Zealand rail.

Opposite:
The best-known locomotive in Wellington during the first twenty-five years of this century was undoubtedly 'Jumbo' the 2-8-4 banking engine of the old Wellington & Manawatu Railway Company. The photo shows Jumbo at Johnsonville in the early years of its career, with the stationmaster prominent in the middle of the group on the platform. The driver is seen to the left, and a guard at the far right holds a tablet for the run back down the hill to Thorndon.

WAIRARAPA MAIL TIMETABLE 1939

HASL	M	Stations	No. 740 Passenger Daily		No. 807 Passenger Daily	
8	—	Wellington (R)	dep	7.50 a.m.	arr	5.44 p.m.
1141	35	Summit	arr	9.41 a.m.	dep	3.59 p.m.
			dep	9.46 a.m.	arr	3.54 p.m.
		Rimutaka Incline				
272	38	Cross Creek	arr	10.06 a.m.	dep	3.17 p.m.
			dep	10.11 a.m.	arr	3.11 p.m.
376	66	Masterton (R)	arr	11.17 a.m.	dep	2.06 p.m.
			dep	11.23 a.m.	arr	1.59 p.m.
261	115	Woodville Jc (R)	arr	1.22 p.m. (f)	dep	12.13 p.m.

CONNECTIONS

HASL	M	Stations		No. 925 Mixed	No. 612 Express	No. 913 Express	No. 922 Mixed
		Woodville Jc	dep	1.55 p.m.	1.31 p.m.	arr 11.55 a.m.	12.00 p.m.
100	133	Palmerston N (R)	arr	2.53 p.m.		dep	11.04 a.m.(b)
10	210	Napier (R)	arr		4.57 p.m.	dep 8.28 a.m.	
						(a)	

(f) = train runs through to Palmerston North (as Mixed); change for Napier.

(a) = change trains.

(b) = runs through to Wairarapa, mixed to Woodville.

(R) = refreshment station.

Part Two: Interlude

The Taumarunui-Marton Mixed passes the second Wellington-Auckland express at Kakahi in December 1909. Both trains are hauled by X class mountain-type engines especially designed for work in this type of rugged country.

Mixed Trains

M ixed trains were once a familiar sight along the NZR from one end to the other. Carrying both passengers and goods, although really more in the nature of goods trains with passenger accomodation, they plied both mainline and humble branchline. On the mainline they catered for the lonely stations ignored by the express trains in their headlong flight, while on the branchlines they often took care of all the regular traffic. A typical timetable provided for morning and afternoon trains in both directions, although a few of the less important lines had only the one train 'single engine in steam' working, even in the days of steam. Recollection of the mixed train usually conjures up a picture of a long rake of goods and stock wagons, with a couple of old-fashioned cars and guard's van rolling along sedately at the rear. Sometimes there would be a roadsider van on the tail for good measure. Up front, the engines were often of a similar vintage to the cars.

When leaving Oamaru on the express in the 1930s I recall being fascinated by the sight of a handsome-looking Baldwin ten-wheeler of 1901 standing outside the locomotive running shed. It was Ub-337, the Kurow branch engine, waiting between trains, and it had to be the cleanest and most polished engine in the South Island at the time. At the other end of the scale there were the Main Trunk mixed trains that ran between the various sub-terminals on the Main Trunk between Palmerston North and Frankton Junction. These trains provided the principal all-year-round daylight services, and were hauled during the last two decades of steam by the modern and powerful K and J classes (with their sub-classes). Overall speeds were somewhat higher at up to 20 m.p.h., and there were as many as three services in each direction between sub-terminals. In winter, the cars were run next to the engines to provide steam heating.

Passengers on the mixed trains were a cross section of country locals, plus a few family or business visitors. At holiday times, the mixed might become a solid passenger train to take people to the races, an A & P Show, a church or school picnic, and the like. Numerous children went to school on the mixed train in the old days. For example, the South Island Working Timetables used to carry a homely footnote for the crew of the Kurow Mixed, advising that Trains Nos. 261 and 272 'will stop opposite Waitaki High School to set down (and pick up) pupils'. In fact, school children became the main source of passenger traffic after the 1920s when the farmers started buying motorcars and bus services were established. A history of the Mt Somers District relates that even in 1921-3 the local stationmaster's wife went into Ashburton for shopping with the wife of a local farmer in the new family car. A competing bus service in this area started in 1925.

Limited to a maximum speed of 30 m.p.h., the mixed train was scarcely the most exhilarating form of travel. There were numerous stops for passengers and shunting en route, which reduced the average overall speed to 14 m.p.h. The old 'hand-me-down' carriages were not all that comfortable either. For a long time, until the 1930s anyway, longitudinal bench seating was the norm. Before first class on the mixed trains was phased out during the Depression, one can recall some vintage cars of Victorian origin which provided for accommodation in four compartments for first and second class, smoking and non-smoking. First class was distinguished by the addition of upholstery at the backs of the seats as well as the seats themselves. Second class backs were T & G wooden lining. Pintsch gas lighting lingered on and there was no steam heat for winter runs (except as previously mentioned on the Main Trunk, and two or three others, all in fairly recent times). The luckier passengers (those in first class) were provided with the famous 'foot warmer', a flat metal can, about two feet long, filled with hot water and some sodium acetate crystals. As the can cooled, a shake would cause it to heat up again temporarily. I remember a trip to Reefton from Greymouth on the early morning mixed in 1928 with my family in a birdcage carriage, to which these footwarmers had been supplied. At the time, I suppose one was much more interested in the Uc class 4-6-0 which powered the train.

For all the tedium, the local people were able to look back on many happy memories of social mixing on the train. It was something of a focal point. An indication of this was seen at Timaru in October 1966 when as many as 142 attended a reunion of 'Fairlie Flyer' ex-pupils. The 'Fairlie Flyer' was the name sentimentally bestowed upon the old branch mixed over its last years. Some of the ex-pupils had travelled to school on it for 11–12 years. One pupil, William Vance, remembers his boyhood days when there was always something interesting to look at while waiting for the train at Fairlie. There was a queue of people waiting to get their tickets, the porter with

A Wayside Vignette:
All dressed up for a winter day in town, two Purakanui women await the arrival of the morning Mixed which will take them into Dunedin and bring them home in the afternoon. The Station Master is all prepared to flag down the train for them. More than likely it will be hauled by an Addington B class 4-8-0 or a Baldwin Q 4-6-2. Purakanui Station, 12 miles from Dunedin and on the north side of the Mihiwaka Tunnel was a tablet station and crossing place during most of its lifetime.
We are grateful to the unknown photographer who captured and preserved this quiet relaxed scene from the railway operation of yesterday. From today's viewpoint we can envy the very human scale of it all.

Nothing could more typify the once all-encompassing role of NZR as a common carrier than this delightfully informal scene of mother, young child and pushcart preparing to board a Blenheim-Picton Mixed (No. 939) at the flag station of Tuamarina on 9 February 1948. The guard, in lay attire, is preparing to unload a milk can before loading the pushcart onto the van. This train was providing an amenity which had then endured for nearly 75 years, and the rolling stock tended to match the longevity of the service. Most of it dates from the turn of the century. The Wf class tank engine goes back to 1905, the J sheep wagons and L open goods wagons considerably pre-date that. The car is an original arch roof model of the lates 1890s and the van dates from the early 1900s.

Timeless Mt Ruapehu dominates the scene in this photo showing a Main Trunk Mixed making a stop at Waiouru. The engine looks like a Bb 4-8-0 of a class built by Price's of Thames between 1915 and 1918. One can only guess that the work-stained railwayman in the foreground was diverted by the photographer while en route to the goods shed on the left. No doubt a welcome incident in the isolation of up country life in those pioneering times on the Trunk; times when the railway was the only practical link with the outside world.

his barrow-load of luggage, pushing his way along the busy platform, the puffing and shunting of the engine; and best of all, the stationmaster ringing the bell at departure time. Travel was a happy family occasion. Everyone knew everyone else, and there was a hum of chatter. But there was not always talking: Mrs Cook of Fairlie liked travelling on the train because it gave her time to think, and other busy people surely felt the same way.

For those who liked railways, there were other compensations, too, in the way of a closer look at the line and the men who manned it. It was diverting to watch the goods wagons being shunted en route, with the guard precariously riding the brake lever on trucks being set down. One could enjoy just loitering about the rural stations. Perhaps there was some loading going on, this being especially interesting when it involved the filling of stock wagons via the station stockyards and races. Or maybe a wagon or two were being unloaded in the lofty corrugated iron goods shed. In days when vandalism was not so rife, it was intriguing to examine the large billboards displaying system timetables and various posters advertising the running of specials to races, shows, school and church picnics, and the like. At Christmas and Easter there would be details of the running of holiday specials.

There was more activity at staffed stations, with their signalling and interlocking systems, and, on the mainline, the elaborate operations connected with the workings of the tablet system. And for good measure, mainline mixed trains usually went into a loop at a staffed station — if only a tablet station manned by a porter — to allow an express to cross. There was a ritual in this, too. Express passengers appeared to look at the mixed in the loop with some disdain as they rolled by in the latest carriages from the NZR workshops.

For all its disadvantages, the mixed train gave long and valuable service to districts where there were not sufficient passengers offering to make a wholly passenger train an economic proposition, even in the days before car and bus competition. As late as 1950 mixed trains were running over one third as many miles as passenger trains proper, including suburbans.

The mixed train came to the end of the line in 1955 when, with little ceremony, this class of train was withdrawn from the timetables. It had become an anachronism in the modern railway scene.

The Railway Station

The railway station was a place of special significance; the starting point of memorable train rides, or a good place just to wander about and watch the comings and goings of the trains and all the kinds of people involved. The railway seemed like another world, another New Zealand, quite separate from the outside, and the station was the entrance to this world. It was a world of the railway carriage, of rights of way removed from public highways and streets for the most part, of the busy stations themselves, and of the railwaymen, a special breed of New Zealanders. In riding the trains one looked through the car windows at the 'outside world' and felt detached from it. Perhaps, this was why so many people found train travel restful.

The railway station was the way you entered this special world, and departed from it. Even in a moderate size station, there were a surprisingly wide variety of the skills and duties necessary to run the trains. Porters, shunters, labourers, train examiners, wagon and car inspectors, signalmen, booking clerks, parcels and luggage clerks, telegraphists, goods clerks, and so on, according to the size of the station. At the head of the team was the stationmaster. Always conspicuous at the departure of the more important passenger trains, he was readily identified by the broad band of gold braid around his peaked cap, and in the bigger stations in pre-war times, by a blue frock coat with large NZR brass buttons. I recall a Mr Fowler, stationmaster at Greymouth in the 1930s, as a wonderful example of the old-time stationmaster, a rather Olympian figure to me, a second-year traffic cadet at the time. More often than not, it was he who rang the station bell for departure, after he had given personal attention to any VIPs who may have been travelling. All this has largely disappeared, long ago. There was seemingly no room for such frills in the post-war railway scene. The decline was marked by such incongruities as stationmasters appearing dressed in sports

Opposite:
Refreshment room girls, charming in their freshly laundered uniforms, pose outside the Clinton Refreshment Rooms in the early years of the century. To their right are the supervisor and the manager. Note the drinking fountain in the centre and the advertisements for firms and products now long-since forgotten. The notice prohibiting smoking on the platform was removed by an edict from Mr Hiley who became General Manager in 1913. A very early concession in permissiveness!

At first sight Invercargill station is a long, rambling, barnlike weatherboard structure much abused by time and the elements, and like many of these structures devoid of architectural merit. Closer inspection, however, reveals some details of considerable quality and charm. The temple-like portico and Queen Anne windows belong to the early station of 1864. Contrast this delicate style to that of the Waimiha Station (below) on the North Island Main Trunk line — functional, perhaps, but less than memorable.

REFRESHMENT-ROOM CHARGES.

Extract from Conditions of Lease.

CLAUSE 5.—" The lessee shall be strictly required to keep and conduct the rooms in a proper and orderly manner, and use his best endeavours for the convenience and accommodation of the public. The list of refreshments and the prices thereof, as specified by the lessee in his tender, and such conditions of this lease as the Minister may think fit, must be exhibited by him in a conspicuous place to the satisfaction of the District Traffic Manager, and the lessee shall keep for sale all the articles mentioned in the schedule at the prices mentioned therein."

SET-TABLE ROOMS.—Frankton Junction, Marton, Woodville, Otira, Oamaru, and Clinton.

At set-table rooms the lessee must, on the arrival and departure of through passenger-trains, have set-table meals ready, as per Schedule No. 1; and will also provide counter refreshments, as per Schedule No. 2, for all trains.

COUNTER REFRESHMENT-ROOMS.—Whangarei, Maungaturoto, Helensville, Mercer, Taumarunui, Ohakune, Taihape, Hawera, Patea, Aramoho, Palmerston North, Waipukurau, Paekakariki, Masterton, Kaitoke, Ikamatua, Moana, Christchurch, Ashburton, Palmerston South, Dunedin, and Gore.

At Christchurch rooms breakfast is obtainable, in addition to counter refreshments.

At the counter refreshment-rooms the lessee must have refreshments provided, as per Schedule No. 2, at convenient hours, to suit the times of arrival and departure of all passenger-trains during the day or night.

SCHEDULE No. 1.

LUNCHEON (SET-TABLE).—BILL OF FARE.—CHARGE, 2s. 6d.

Soup (or Fish) and Hot Joint.—Beef, mutton, lamb, or pork; also potatoes, with some other vegetable in season; fresh white bread; butter and cheese, and marmalade; salad, pickles, lettuce, celery, or tomatoes; and a large cup of tea or coffee.

In lieu of the joint, either chops, steaks, ham and eggs, sausages, preserved fish, or cold ham must be supplied when ordered.

Serviettes, either of linen or paper.

A hot joint must be on the table on the arrival of the through passenger-trains, and the other articles in lieu thereof must be in readiness; and the lessee will have to provide attendants to carve expeditiously, and wait upon the passengers.

At Otira the charge for luncheon (set table) will be 3s.

On Lake Wakatipu steamers the charge for meals (set table) will be 3s.; morning or afternoon tea, 1s.

SCHEDULE No. 2.

COUNTER REFRESHMENTS.

Sandwiches (ham, tongue, beef, mince, or egg), half of full slice over large size sandwich loaf ..	4d.	Bread (full slice over large size sandwich loaf), roll, scone, or bun, with butter	4d.
Tea, coffee, cocoa (with milk and sugar), or milk, large cup ..	4d.	Block cake (not less than 2½ oz.) or small cakes of equal weight ..	4d.
Aerated waters (consumed at counter), per bottle or glass ..	6d.	Milk and sodawater, per glass ..	6d.

Cordials, &c., not enumerated, to be charged at the same rate per bottle and glass as at the principal hotels in the Dominion.

The lessee is bound by the terms of his lease to supply articles of the best description only, and passengers who consider they have reason to complain should do so to the Stationmaster. Clear and pure drinking-water, properly filtered, is to be supplied, free of charge, to all railway travellers.

Refreshments can also be obtained at the following stations, viz.: Towai, Putaruru, Paeroa, Te Awamutu, Te Kuiti, Raurimu, Mataroa, Te Karaka, Tadmor, Rangiora, Waipara, Springfield, Hindon, Omakau, Milton, Houipapa, Winton, and Lumsden, These rooms and stalls are, however, held under different conditions from those mentioned above. At Ranfurly refreshments can be obtained opposite the station.

Inside the Dining Room at Clinton railway station. This inviting scene awaits hungry passengers, and reflects the dignity and opulence of the Edwardian era. The wooden tongue-and-groove linings of the time make a background for such typical decorative items as the stag's head, the gilt framed paintings, the handsome dresser, and the impressive brass lamp.

coats and trousers, and even sandals, topped off with a gold-braided cap!

To the prospective passenger, the booking hall, often sharing functions with the main waiting room, was the focal point of the station. If it was a somewhat austere place with its tongue and groove wood linings, scrubbed wooden floors, wood seat benches, old rail hearth fender and the low netting grill ticket window, all this was overshadowed by colorful posters inviting you to cross the Rockies on the famous Canadian Pacific Railway, to visit lovely Torquay on the Great Western Railway of England, or to travel across the Nullabor Plain on the Trans-Australian Railway. The walls of the booking office and station were also screened by numerous familiar trade advertisements relating to very wide range of products from Beechams Famous Liver Pills to Old Judge Cigarettes ('You can't beat 'em'), K Jams, and Pear's Soap (the latter with the reproduction of Sir William Orpen's famous painting of the boy blowing bubbles). A lot of wall space was also covered by the system timetables for both islands and notices of forthcoming specials, all prominently displayed on huge NZR notice boards. Your journey ticket would be selected from a large rack of pasteboard tickets for a myriad of destinations and date-stamped with a resounding thump, or thumps in the case of a return ticket. You grasped the precious bit of paste board in your hand and moved out towards the platform and train with pleasurable anticipation. Or better still, in the case of a through station, you were able to anticipate the train's arrival with some delight before it actually bustled in, and you joined the scramble for a good seat on the sunny side or the scenic side of the train, or better still, both.

A Magnificent Station

When it was built in 1904, Dunedin's railway station was acclaimed as the finest in New Zealand. Today, over seventy years later, and notwithstanding newer stations in the other three main cities, it is still regarded as the finest in the country.

The station was designed by Sir George Troup, design engineer with New Zealand railways, in a style appropriately described as 'Flemish Renaissance'. Undoubtedly it is architecture in the romantic tradition; with its noble tower, its dramatic contrasts of form and colour, and its gay yet dignified decorative pattern. If there was once a certain grandness about train travel, then this station seemed to symbolise the idea.

There was a similar sort of impact inside the building. Passengers passed from the portico into a lofty and spacious booking hall with a balustraded gallery encircling it. The booking windows are set in rich Baroque decoration in white terra cotta, while the floor is surfaced with a beautiful

George Troup's elaborate 1904 design for the present Dunedin Railway Station.

The magnificent booking hall at Dunedin's Railway Station, part of George Troup's very elaborate design. Note the NZR motifs in the floor mosaic and over the door and ticket windows.

and intricate mosaic incorporating locomotive motifs and NZR monograms.

Less is heard about the operating side of the station, but this aspect is equally impressive. The main platform is the longest and widest in the country. The main platform has cross-overs and is the equivalent of two platforms. Most of the platform area is covered by an enormous shelter supported by an elaborate system of steel trussing with a very dramatic vista effect.

The period 1900-1950 is seen as the golden age of the passenger train. At the beginning of the period, the passenger train had reached a comparatively mature stage of development, and over the ensuing fifty years enjoyed an all-time peak of patronage.

The Dunedin Station saw and coped with all these busy passenger years. On a typical weekday in the mid-1930s, for example, there were seventy-five passenger-train movements in and out of the station — approximately eleven every hour. From the opening of the station until about 1920 the famous Baldwin Q's, with some assistance from the Ub's, held the limelight as they worked these trains in and out of Dunedin. In the 1920s and 1930s the standard era Ab express engines and their Wab tank engine offshoots were used. In 1930, the familiar wooden-bodied open-platform cars gave way to glamorous steel-panelled cars with closed vestibules on the through trains. Modernity arrived at the station in 1940 in the form of the North British streamstyled J class engines, and the big 56 ft 'bullet' carriages, the future standard express cars for the whole NZR. The South Island Limited replaced the traditional express trains in 1949, about which time the locally built Ja's were taking over the mainline workings. But post-war the drift had set in, and the station became increasingly quieter with the dismal cycle of fewer passengers and fewer trains. Today, the only mainline passenger train using the station is the Southerner. Apart from this there is only a remnant of the Mosgiel suburban service.

World Wars I and II were times of exceptional activity at the station with the greatly swollen loads on the mainline services and many troop specials operating, but probably the greatest traffic peaks ever experienced occurred during the New Zealand and South Seas Exhibition, held at Dunedin in 1925-26. Nearly a quarter of a million visitors came to Dunedin by train to see the big show, all using the station on their arrival and departure. On one busy day, 10 April 1926, 5,000 passengers arrived from the north in eight trains.

There were also the race specials (Wingatui was a favourite place), the Sunday excursions to Timaru and places like the Catlins, the Blossom Festival Specials (to Alexandra), the Daffodil Specials (to Lawrence), and of course the football specials.

Part Three: The South Island

The Picton Express with an Ab engine, four cars and two vans, steaming out of the old Christchurch station on a dull wet winter morning in 1948. A clear signal is showing for the No. 2 bay platform from which the express started. The other signal is for the main platform occupied by the South Express due out at 8.35 a.m. This photo captures No. 104's engine bumping over the twin tram tracks on the very busy Colombo Street crossing. Christchurch was unique for its railway-tramway crossings. Tram routes were protected by railway-type semaphore signals and catch points operated from signal cabins adjoining the crossings.

The Picton Express

As late as the 1930s, trains travelled north of Christchurch only to Parnassus — a distance of eighty miles, the end of the line. For many years the section from Waipara to Parnassus was known as the Cheviot Branch, with the main passenger service going to Waiau, and part of this train running to Parnassus. In the mid-1920s, the Parnassus train became the main service north, and was singled out for the first trial of the new 'Midland Red' carriage colour scheme, to replace the rather drab olive green with yellow trim which had prevailed for a very long time. The term Midland Red derived from the fact that this colour was well known as the standard livery for engines and carriages of the Midland Railway in England.

The through Picton Express service (Trains Nos. 104 and 109) was inaugurated in December 1945 upon completion of the so-called South Island Main Trunk. This long awaited express service promised a new era in travel to Marlborough and offered an alternative crossing to the North Island by the ferry from Picton to Wellington. But the share of inter-island passenger traffic was disappointing, and Nos. 104 and 109 were never much more than modest provincial expresses and as such were the shortest lived in New Zealand, being replaced by railcars in February 1956.

Clouds were already beginning to gather on the horizon even when the new trains commenced running. Only a month later, in January 1946, serious coal shortages forced a cut from the planned daily service to Monday-Wednesday-Friday which endured over the remaining life of the trains (excepting for holiday times). With the 1950s and the ever mounting road and air competition patronage dwindled. Despite its wonderful scenic attractions the route never became a practical choice for the majority of inter-island surface travellers who continued to favour the convenience and cheaper fares of the long established steamer express route from Lyttelton. In fact, the 1950 timetable, for example, did not even refer to inter-island connections. However, the expresses carried hundreds of thousands of passengers in their brief ten-year career, and those who made the trip were well rewarded by the magnificent coastal scenery seen over so much of the run.

A coastal route always has a special appeal to the traveller. On railways around the world there are renowned coastal runs of sustained length. In Europe the most fascinating is the route of the former Paris, Lyons and Mediterranean Railway along the Côte d'Azur through Nice and Cannes on the northern shores of the Mediterranean Sea. This was the route of the famous 'Blue Train', well known in film and novel. In America the most notable stretch of coastal railway is on the San Francisco-Los Angeles 'Coast Route' of the Southern Pacific Railroad, where the line runs for hundreds of miles alongside the Pacific Ocean. Before the days of the jet plane and the motorway it was the route of what has been called America's most beautiful steam train, 'The Coast Daylight'.

TIMETABLE CHRISTCHURCH-PICTON EXPRESS 1950

HASL	M	Stations	No. 109 M.W.F.	No. 104 M.W.F.
18	—	Christchurch	dep 8.25 a.m.	arr 6.07 p.m.
235	41	Waipara (R)	dep 9.48 a.m.	dep 4.49 p.m.
—	120	Kaikoura (R)	dep 12.58 p.m.	dep 1.38 p.m.
15	200	Blenheim*	dep 4.05 p.m.	dep 10.35 a.m.
10	218	Picton	arr 4.40 p.m.	dep 9.45 p.m.

(* Road connection Nelson)
(R = refreshment station)

The Picton Express following the picturesque Kaikoura coast.

S.S. Wahine on arrival at Picton on New Year's Day 1930, after running the traditional excursion from Wellington to the Picton Regatta. The connecting train for Blenheim is seen on the right. The Wahine was a Wellington-Lyttleton inter-island steamer, but was used on this excursion because it had a larger capacity than the usual Wellington-Picton steamer, the Tamahine.

The Christchurch-Culverden Express derailed on Death's Corner near Sefton, 16 October 1907

In our own country, the run down the Kaikoura Coast can rank in the same category. Other notable coastal runs in New Zealand such as Paekakariki, Blueskin Bay near Dunedin, and the coastal stretches between Wairoa and Gisborne are nowhere near as sustained, nor do they contain the same scale of engineering works.

The Picton Line runs along the coast for about sixty miles. There are seventeen tunnels through the stark bluffs, a unique feature being a 'barrel' tunnel in the open, linking two ordinary tunnels, to protect the line against slips. Large ventilation slots were made in the seaward side of this tunnel enabling passengers to enjoy the unique experience of seeing the sea from a tunnel. As well as the tunnels there are numerous bridges near the mouths of rivers and streams, the Clarence and the Hapuka bridges being very impressive structures.

A curiosity of the Picton Line is the fact that it has been always referred to as the South Island Main Trunk. No doubt, the original notion was that this line was the uncompleted portion of a South Island Main Trunk line running from Invercargill to Picton. But it did not remain that way. The Picton line itself became known as the South Island Main Trunk, while the Invercargill-Christchurch line retained the popular name of 'the South Island Main Line.' In fact the latter is more truly the trunk line. To further complicate things, the line to Parnassus was, as we have noted, once called the Cheviot Branch.

The Culverden Express

The *Canterbury Times* of 16 October 1907 contained an interesting account of a minor mishap to the Culverden-Christchurch Express:

> The express train from Culverden last Thursday, consisting of four cars, a mail van and two luggage vans, drawn by locomotive No. 284, had a narrow escape from a serious accident. Running down the incline south of Balcairn Station at considerable but not more than ordinary speed on to the sharp curve near Sefton known as Death's Corner, the two front wheels of the bogie on the locomotive left the metals at the road crossing in the centre of the curve. The engine-driver promptly applied the Westinghouse brake, with sand on the rails, and pulled up the train before it had travelled more than double its own length. Fortunately the other wheels of the bogie kept on the metals, otherwise the train would almost inevitably have gone off the line into a deep depression beside it. Seeing that the derailed wheels travelled over a cattle stop and a culvert several feet in length it is little short of miraculous that the accident was not more serious.

Although only a minor affair, the rarity of such a happening made it newsworthy. Throughout the long history of passenger operation on this line not a single passenger was even injured. But from our point of view the incident was fortuitous in producing an extremely rare photograph of the so-called express which was the most important passenger train operating in North Canterbury for many years subsequent to the opening of the line over the Weka Pass to Culverden in 1886.

At one time this line with its Waiau extension was seen as the prospective main route to the provinces of Nelson and Marlborough in the north. It appears that the Culverden Express enjoyed a share of the most modern equipment of the day. Engine No. 284 was a Ub class Baldwin ten-wheeler of 1899 and the leading type of express engine in Canterbury, and with the exception of the front postal car, a conversion from an old clerestory roof car of the 1880s, all the carriages are contemporary express vehicles. The first and last are mainline cars of the early 1900s, with in between a 'birdcage' and an American compartment car.

Ab-748 rumbles over the girders of the new Wairau River bridge with the Picton Express on 11 February 1948. The Wairau River, originating deep in the mountains of Marlborough, is the province's major river, and the line crosses it just beyond Tuamarina, about five miles from Blenheim.
The new bridge replaced the old wooden structure that served the Picton-Blenheim line from its opening in 1875.

A southbound Picton Express leaves Seddon, headed by an Ab engine. The size of the train, three cars and some roadsider wagons, indicates that this is the off season.

Above halfway down the Mihiwaka Bank the main-line runs through the curved MacGregor Tunnel which pierced a sizeable rock escarpment. No. 145 is seen flowing out of the tunnel on 23 March 1942 with its double-heading engines assuming a counter cant on the tight reverse curve leading into the deep rocky cutting in the fore-ground. The exit from the MacGregor Tunnel was about as crammed a piece of line as could be found anywhere. In a situation like this there was little more than enough room for the carriages, and some-times overhanging branches of manuka and other growth might even brush against a window.

The South Express

Without a doubt, the best known and most prestigious passenger trains of the South Island system during the Golden Age of Steam were the Christchurch-Invercargill Expresses, No. 145 and 174, both popularly known in Canterbury simply as the 'South Expresses'. No. 174 was also called the 'Boat Express' or 'Ferry Express' because of its direct connection at the Lyttelton Wharf with the inter-island ferry.

The South Express was a train with a long history, with origins back as far as 1878. There was an aura of tradition about it; the evolution of its equipment was largely the story of railway technology on the NZR and several generations of staff were concerned with the operation of the train. The South Express was New Zealand's first express train, and preceded the Main Trunk service in the North Island by thirty years — years of the general ascendancy of the South Island, when much of Main Trunk country was an uninhabited wilderness and the Auckland-Wellington railway a dream of the future.

The South Express had a reputation for fast-running across the Canterbury Plains. When talk got around to train travel there was always someone ready to tell about his latest, fastest trip over the plains on the express. It is even reported that an American K attained speeds of up to 55 mph on the inaugural journey between Christchurch and Dunedin. In the Ab era speeds in the upper fifties were quite common with peaks in the mid-sixties, especially on the last stage of the journey from Rakaia to the outskirts of Christchurch. These speeds made for exhilarating travelling and memorable trips.

Although the through line from Christchurch to Invercargill was opened in 1879, the year following the Christchurch-Dunedin opening, it was not until 1904 that expresses were run right through in a single day. Previously there had been an overnight stay at Dunedin and through-passengers continued next morning on another train. Nos. 145 and 174 emerged as the major through-expresses, and they dominated trunk route travel in the South Island for many decades. In their heyday they carried something like 250,000 passengers a year.

The South Express bestrode the South Island Main Line like a friendly giant. It became one of the South Island's deepest-rooted public institutions. There was drama in its comings and goings, which were closely interwoven with the daily life of on-line communities in a way unknown to present day transport. There were few people then who did not have some personal contact with the express in one way or another, travelling on it, farewelling family or friends, or simply seeing it go through town. Governors-General, rugby teams, cricket teams, politicians, and all kinds of celebrities and near celebrities were welcomed and farewelled as they arrived and departed.

The passage of the South Expresses up and down the line was not unlike a triumphal procession, with the crowds thronging the platforms at stopping places, and the railway staffs ever alert to prompt servicing to ensure an uninterrupted path ahead. At least one General Manager demanded the running reports of the expresses promptly on his desk every day for personal inspection.

Everything gave way to the express. Only the best engines and the most senior crews were used on these runs — and the engine and cars were always given that extra ounce of spit and polish. Their drivers could even become public personalities, like well-known driver Richard Stone of the Linwood Depot in the 1920s, who drove the Royal Trains and was featured in the press as the driver of Ab 608 Paschendaele. J.M. Grainger in his book *On and Off the Rails* says this about Driver Stone: 'In any large organisation there are men who, although doing exactly the same work as their companions, achieve a distinction which puts them in a class by themselves. One such person was the late Richard Stone. When I was a boy he was my hero. My first scrapbook included several photographs cut from local newspapers with engine driver Stone at the controls of some special train run for some V.I.P. He had retired before I ever started as a cleaner, but his exploits and reputation live on.'

Nos. 145 and 174 were, of all express trains, the most closely identified with the inimitable Ab engine, which was the standard power throughout the 1920s and 1930s (except for the Oamaru-Dunedin section where the running was shared with Wab's, which were really Ab engines converted into tank engines). It was with Nos. 145 and 174 on the Canterbury Plains that the Ab's built up their astonishing reputation for fast running. Perhaps the most thrilling of all my railway memories is seeing No. 174 go through Rolleston one fine summer evening in 1933. I was travel-

Christchurch 'that most English of New Zealand cities' gains much of its character from its fine old Gothic Buildings like the cathedral, and the old railway station was a picturesque structure in the same tradition, fitting perfectly into its city setting. It was built in 1877 and served Christ-church for about three-quarters of a century before it was replaced by the present modern struc-ture in 1960. This photo shows the South Express on arrival at Christchurch in charge of an N class Baldwin locomotive of 1885.

The South Express gathering speed as it draws out of the Christchurch station yard and clatters over the tramline crossings in Colombo Street, in the late 1920s.

ling to Greymouth on the 'Perishable' and we had stopped at Rolleston to let the express go through. After a while there was a hum in the rails which mounted until the express itself, doubleheaded, came into view. It seemed incredible that a train could move so fast. There was a slight wobble of the engines as they swept over the junction crossovers, and after that there was just a blurred impression of swaying pitching engines and rocketing cars. Passengers were sensed rather than seen. The exhausts of the two engines merged into one deep continuous roar. The speed must have been well into the sixties. It was all over in a matter of seconds, but the memory of it all has lasted for years. The 'Perishable' seemed slower than ever when it resumed its run.

The Development of the South Express

The South Express first appeared in 1878 during the height of the great Victorian railway age when railways were fast expanding everywhere in the world and bringing about a new era in commerce and travel. It was New Zealand's first express train, and until the inauguration of the Main Trunk services between Wellington and Auckland in 1909 it was the only trunk line express. As such it became a great South Island community institution over generations of popular and reliable service, and built up a tradition beyond that of any other New Zealand train. The story of its evolution reflects the progress of NZR passenger train technology, a tale as interesting and varied as any found on railways anywhere in the world.

In spite of the strong ties of Empire felt in New Zealand during these colonial days, there was tremendous rivalry between British and American influences in locomotive and passenger car design. With the support of A.D. Smith, an American who became first Locomotive Superintendent (1878-85), American design soon became uppermost. The locomotives and cars were much more suited to the lighter and less perfectly aligned tracks of the economically-built colonial railways.

The lingering impression of the South Express over the Victorian era is that of American Rogers and Baldwin-built engines clickety-clacking over the Canterbury Plains with their smoke trailing over the roofs of imposing American-style bogie 'palace cars', either built in that country or at the local Addington workshops to American designs. Further, the trains ran on American-style flat-bottom rails distinct from the bull-head type universally used on British mainline railways. However, about the turn of the century, a distinctively native New Zealand style began to emerge with the standard Mainline arch roof wooden cars with their narrow T & G sheathing, and 'Addington' engine designs such as the U class 4-6-0's and the A class 4-6-2 compounds, both incorporating elements of American and British practice.

The following summary sets out the historical pattern of the main locomotives and cars used on the South Express over its lengthy years of operation. The dates indicate the introduction of new equipment, but it will be appreciated that the full changeover could take some time, perhaps years in the case of new locomotives. For example, although Ab engines were introduced in 1915, at the end of 1920 there were only nine at work in the South Island, so that old engines could be sharing the working of the train over several years. Old hands recall U's and Ub's working the express between Timaru and Oamaru until after 1920, and an old driver, 'Gentleman John', remembered driving a Ub between these two places with the southbound express as late as 1930, although this would have been an exceptional occurrence.

The timetable of the South Express at the time of its inauguration in September 1878 provided for an overall journey time of 11 hr 5 mins for the 230-mile run to Dunedin, this being adjusted to 10 hr 55 min (21.1 mph) the following year, with a net time of 9½ hrs (24.2 mph). The train left Christchurch at 8.40 a.m. and arrived at Dunedin at 7.35 p.m. and there were only eight intermediate stops. As pioneer expresses, and especially in the light of subsequent events, these trains were real fliers. There was a speed limit of 30 mph. Speed had to be kept down to 12-15 mph on the bridges, and the hill country south of Oamaru with its numerous 1 in 50 grades and 7½-chain curves did not encourage high speed either. Nevertheless the American K enginnes could run very comfortably on the heavier rail at 45 mph, and on occasion the time was cut from the 9½ hrs to under 9 hrs. For example, a North Express of nine to ten cars hauled by a single K and assisted by an F (from Dunedin to Palmerston) and a T (from Palmerston to Oamaru) was timed at 8 hr 56 mins. The T's did some remarkable work on the expresses. As 2-8-0 engines with 3 ft driving wheels they were designed for drag work on goods trains, but showed they could run quite smoothly on the passenger trains at 30 mph.

All this was too good to last. So often in NZR affairs, a period of advancement was followed by one of retrenchment. And so, in 1880 with the onset of depression, the South Express was turned into something like an ordinary stopping train over most of the run in an effort to replace cancelled trains. Some fifty to sixty stops (many optional) were included in the timetable and the overall time expanded to 12 hr 5 mins. Strict orders were given that the maximum speed was not to exceed 25 m.p.h. in any circumstances. The economy timetable provided for a Christchurch departure of 8.20 a.m. and a Dunedin arrival at 8.25 p.m. Public reaction was most adverse, and as a result of political pressure the time was tightened in 1881 from 12 hr 5 mins to 11 hr 20 mins — leaving Christchurch at 8 a.m. and arriving in Dunedin at 7.40 p.m. Many stops were eliminated, only three being retained between Oamaru and Dunedin, but there were still eight between Christchurch and Ashburton.

CHRISTCHURCH – DUNEDIN – INVERCARGILL EXPRESS TRAINS.

DOWN.

Wellington } steamer { dep 7.45 p.m. daily except Sunday.
Lyttelton .. } express { arr 7 a.m. next morning.

Lyttelton (Wharf) dep } Special train leaves Lyttelton for Christchurch after arrival of steamer express. Breakfast obtainable at Christchurch Railway Refreshment-rooms immediately on arrival of train
Christchurch arr }

		am	Mon. am	Tu. W. Th. F. Sat. am	Sun. pm	W. F. pm	Sun. pm
CHRISTCHURCH	dep	..	8 35	8 35	..	12 25	11 2 Mon. am
TIMARU	dep	..	11 50	11 33	..	3 46	2 2
OAMARU	arr	..	pm 1 30	pm 12 56 Dinner	..	5 26 Tea	3 25
OAMARU	dep	..	1 55	1 19	..	5 49	3 40
DUNEDIN	arr	..	5 1	4 18	..	8 54	6 53
DUNEDIN	dep	8 33	..	4 40	5 30	..	..
MILTON	dep	9 44	..	5 54	6 42	..	..
BALCLUTHA	dep	10 25	..	6 23	7 13	..	..
GORE	dep	pm 12 3	..	7 53	8 59	..	..
INVERCARGILL	arr	1 10	..	9 5	10 3	..	..

CONNECTING TRAINS.
From Gore to Queenstown.

			M. W. F. pm
Gore	..	dep	12 45
Lumsden	..	dep	2 37
Kingston	..	arr	4 16
Kingston	(st'r)	dep	4 30
Queenstown		arr	6 45

For intermediate times, see pages 125–130 (Christchurch-Dunedin); 138–141 (Dunedin-Invercargill); 148, 152, 153 (Gore-Kingston).

UP.

		M, W, F. am	Tu. W. Th, F. Sat. am	pm	Sun. pm
INVERCARGILL	dep	..	7 0	1 45	6 40
GORE	dep	..	8 14	2 59	7 55
BALCLUTHA	dep	..	9 43	4 36	9 22
MILTON	dep	..	10 25	5 13	9 58
DUNEDIN	arr	..	11 29	6 23	10 57
DUNEDIN	dep	8 45	11 35	..	11 20 Mon. am
OAMARU	arr	11 45 pm Dinner	2 37 Dinner	..	2 25
OAMARU	dep	12 8	3 9	..	2 35
TIMARU	dep	1 54	4 34	..	4 18
CHRISTCHURCH	arr	5 10	7 25	..	7 18

CONNECTING TRAINS.
From Queenstown to Gore.

			M, W, F. am
Queenstown	(st'r)	dep	8 25
Kingston		arr	10 5
Kingston	..	dep	11 5
Lumsden	..	dep	pm 1 4
Gore	..	arr	2 35

For fares between the principal stations of the Dominion, see page 23.

Christchurch .. dep daily, 7.10 p.m.; Tu, W, Th, F, Sat, 7.37 p.m.
Lyttelton (Wharf) arr daily, 7.29 p.m.; Tu, W, Th, F, Sat, 7.56 p.m.

Lyttelton } Steamer { dep Mon. about 7.45 p.m.; Tu, W, Th, F, Sat, about 8.10 p.m.; arr 7 a.m
Wellington } express { next morning. Connecting trains go alongside steamers at Lyttelton.

The information in regard to the inter-Island steamer express services is supplied for the benefit of the public, and the Railway Department is not responsible for the operation of the steamer express services.

Timetable – September 1935

American Rogers K engine and British J on train of early British cars and American clerestory bogie cars at Timaru in 1880. Although the train is a summer excursion from Christchurch, the locomotives and cars are the same as those used for the South Express service during the early 1880s. Inexplicably, no good photo of the actual pioneer South Express appears to have survived, a fact which makes this photo invaluable in giving us an accurate idea of what the train actually looked like.

Train time at Milton, 1910. The express is stopped well forward of the station to clear the Invercargill mail train travelling in the opposite direction to allow access by passengers. The engine number 340 is encircled by the inscription 'Baldwin Locomotive Works, Philadelphia, USA'.

This timetable continued with minor changes, until the early 1890s when there was a further substantial cut to 10 hrs journey time (23 m.p.h.) — leaving Christchurch at 11 a.m. and arriving at Dunedin at 9.00 p.m. By now the heavier 53lb rail had been installed throughout, bridges improved, and more powerful engines were in use — the Baldwin N's in Canterbury and the English-built V's in Otago.

At the turn of the century the introduction of much more powerful Baldwins throughout the route — Ub's in Canterbury, and Q's and Ub's in Otago — together with the installation of air-brakes, brought a further trip reduction to 9 hr 15 mins (24.9 m.p.h.).

A major event was the inauguration of a one-day through express service between Christchurch and Invercargill on 1 November 1904. This new South Express ran on Tuesdays, Thursdays and Saturdays — departing Christchurch at 10.10 a.m. and arriving in Invercargill at 12.55 a.m. with an overall time of 14 hr 45 mins (25 m.p.h.). The north-bound express left Invercargill at 8 a.m. and arrived at Christchurch correspondingly earlier. Soon the southbound express departure was altered to 8 a.m. even though it meant losing the steamer connection. However, by 1907 the steamer arrived sufficiently early to connect with the express.

On Mondays, Wednesdays and Fridays a mainline service to Dunedin only was provided by the Dunedin Mail, which left Christchurch at 12.20 p.m. and arrived in Dunedin at 9.25 p.m., with a corresponding northbound service.

The inauguration of the North island Main Trunk express service in February 1909 meant that the Christchurch-Invercargill route was no longer New Zealand's only trunk line. Henceforth it would be seen, together with the inter-island ferries, as part of a national trunk system. There were considerable timetable reorganisations throughout the NZR following this development, and in the case of the South Express many stops were eliminated so that from 1 April 1909 the journey time was cut to 13 hr 12 mins overall (28 m.p.h.). The North Express left Invercargill at 6.15 a.m. to connect with the ferry steamer and next day's Wellington-Auckland Express. With minor adjustments, this timetable remained in force until the big system-wide speed-up of 1925, immediately prior to which the overall time had been eased to 13 hr 25 mins (27.5 m.p.h.).

The only break in the continuous service of the South Express during the whole of its ten years of operation occurred when it was withdrawn between 1917 and 1919 as a wartime measure. The dining car, however, was never reinstated.

By 1925, 70lb rails were standard throughout the mainline tracks, and there was an ample roster of capable, modern Ab-class express engines available at all the main engine depots. At the same time highway competition was starting to make itself really felt. It was time to make the train schedules more competitive with a wholesale speed-up throughout the system. The journey time of the South Express was cut from 13 hr 25 mins to 12 hr 5 mins (30.4 m.p.h.) — leaving Christchurch at 8.50 a.m. and arriving in Invercargill at 8.55 p.m. There were the inevitable second-thought easings. In the mid-thirties the standard schedule was Christchurch depart 8.35 a.m. and Invercargill arrive 9.9 p.m. making 12 hr 30 min overall (25.4 m.p.h.). Apart from some adjustment to meet wartime steamer sailings, this was the basic schedule over the remaining life of the South Express until it was superseded by the South Island Limited in August 1949. A copy of a summary of the 1935 timetable taken from the Public Timetable is reproduced opposite. It was the timetable covering most of the journeys made by the author and other people for whom in the last years of the pre-motor age the express was an indispensable link with a pattern of life that has now disappeared.

Perhaps the finest hour of the South Express was in 1930 when it was re-equipped with brand new carriages of the very latest design. These cars were a radical advance on the traditional open platform wooden-bodied mainline cars they superseded, in that they were steel panelled and had closed vestibules with covered concertina connections between cars. Also they were roomier being 8ft 5 in wide and 50 ft long compared with 7 ft 10 ins and 47½ ft of the mainline cars. Apart from these basic changes the cars incorporated such up-to-the-minute accessories as automatic couplers, fabricated steel bogies of a new design, and roller bearings. They were good-looking cars even by world standards, with pleasing proportions, nicely rounded contours and a single fascia between the roof and the window line. Fanlights, plate glass drop windows, and decorative oval leaded end windows gave a touch of elegance, as did the beautiful gleaming red enamel finish, the gold lettering, the chromium-plated handrails and other fittings. On every trip freshly laundered white headslips were attached to each first-class seat. Cleaned and polished with loving care, the trains were a picture to behold, and the staff were proud of them in a way difficult to visualise nowadays. The later — and last — re-equipment in 1939 with the current 56 ft cars did not have the same impact, these cars being more in the way of an evolution in design, and, from the point of view of the second-class passenger, a retrograde step in that the four abreast seating adopted was less comfortable than the earlier three abreast. The 1939 cars were only 6 ins wider.

The South Express is now becoming a fairly distant memory. The Ab and Ja locomotives that worked it during its last years have long since been scrapped, except for a few preservations. Some of the 56 ft cars display remarkable longevity, still being in use in an upgraded form on the present day diesel-hauled 'Southerner', and on the odd extra run. A few of the glamorous 1930

Train No. 174, the Invercargill-Lyttelton Express, runs into the impressive Gothic portal of the Cliffs Tunnel sometime in 1938, the usual Wab and Ab engines producing the tractive power up front.

The trailing streamer of white exhaust floating low over the countryside marked the passage of the steam passenger train on the South Island mainline for well over a century. It became almost as much part of the landscape as the passing clouds in the sky. The photo depicts a winter scene at Waikouaiti with the cottonwool exhausts of the J and Ab engines working the northbound express streamed behind in a state of virtual suspension in the cold atmosphere.

cars linger on in a very tired and worn-looking state. The author remembers seeing a couple in recent times on the surviving Rangiora local.

However, the train is assured of a permanent and prominent place in the history of South Island railways. Those who can remember travelling on it during its great pre-war days will never forget the experience, or the daily drama that attended the train's comings and goings. It is sad to think that we will never hear again the urgent wail of No. 174 up from the South on a winter's evening as its travel-stained Ab called for the crossings into Christchurch. Ahead was the thronged Christchurch station, and then the steamer connection at Lyttelton for Wellington and the North Island. There are memories too of No. 145 southbound leaving Christchurch on a frosty morning, with its glistening black engine and the contrasting clouds of purest white steam, carefully stepping over the terminal layout before lining up on the multi-track straight way leading to the edge of the horizon beyond suburban Addington.

We can recall the highlights of the train's career, in particular, the beautiful Edwardian version of the train with the classic A engines, stately mainline cars and elegant dining-car service. The train had come of age. We think of it in the gloomy days of World War I and the thousands of soldiers in lemon squeezer hats it carried, followed by the boom years of the 1920s when passenger carrying reached record peaks for peacetime. Traffic was boosted during these years, too, by the record number of passengers carried in connection with the New Zealand and South Seas Exhibition at Dunedin in 1925-6 when a quarter of a million of people are estimated to have travelled to Dunedin. Soon after the elaborate re-equipping in 1930 there was the setback of the Great Depression when passenger loadings became thinner than at any time in living memory. Often a single Wab was all that was needed for the hard Oamaru-Dunedin run, a traditional double-heading stint. Passenger traffic built up again as conditions improved after the mid-1930s, but an event occurred in 1936 which was eventually to have a profound effect on the South Express and its successors — the inauguration of the Union Airways service between the main centres. Union Airways was the forerunner of National Airways and Air New Zealand. Passenger traffic rose to all-time records with World War II and the vast numbers of servicemen and women as well as the severe petrol restrictions. But it was at the price of lowered standards of maintenance and service. The old time gloss and institutional pride disappeared for good, and the few remaining post-war years to 1949 were shadowed by shortages of men and materials and a malaise that had enveloped the railway passenger business. So one likes to remember the South Express as it was in its heyday of the pre-war era — stylish, proud and seemingly invulnerable.

A pleasing rear overhead view of the northbound curving around the landward perimeter of the gardens at Timaru's Caroline Bay taken on 2 January 1915. Judging by the rather limp exhaust of the A class engine, the driver is taking things fairly easily around the Bay, giving the passengers a good opportunity to take a last look at the sea.

Dunedin Station, Christmas Eve 1939. A monster Relief Express for Christchurch, due away shortly after 9.00 a.m., awaits the 'right-away!' In spite of Dunedin's main platform being the longest in the country, the train spills out well in front of the departure signals seen above the second and third cars. Note the exhortation in bold print on the engines side tanks to BUY NZ MADE GOODS, a reminder that foreign exchange crises and the need to conserve overseas funds are nothing new in New Zealand. What was new, not only here but in the world generally, was the use of railway locomotives for advertising.

THE BOAT TRAIN

A familiar sight to passengers on the overnight ferry from Wellington, when the boat berthed at Lyttelton, was the boat train waiting on the wharf to take them through the Lyttelton tunnel to Christchurch. Boat trains have always had a special glamour about them, and trains such as the 'Golden Arrow' between London and Dover were world-famous.

The only other service of comparable importance to the Lyttelton boat train in Australasia was the Hobart-Launceston boat trains of the Tasmanian Railways, which connected with the ferry for Melbourne. There was also the Blenheim-Picton boat train connecting with the ferry from Picton to Wellington, but this was a much more modest operation. Train and steamer travel seemed to complement each other admirably — both were mass carriers, each dominant in its own element; and both were steampowered.

The evening workings were perhaps the most interesting. Somehow the anticipation of the boat journey ahead rather than behind gave more piquancy. Two trains ran direct to the boat in the evening: the Boat Train, departing Christchurch at 7.10 p.m. (in 1950) and the Invercargill-Lyttelton Wharf Express (Train No. 174) which left Christchurch at 7.37 p.m. Neither of these trains stopped en route.

There was an imbalance working between morning and evening, but railway operations always had their share of eccentricities. It was pleasant to travel down on the earlier train — we will always remember the carnival atmosphere of the lights of Lyttelton town and the ships in port — to watch the express rumble on to the wharf backwards, postal van and guard's van leading, in charge of the usual F class engine. On one such occasion in March 1930 Train No. 174 made an unforgettable sight. The then brand-new steel-panelled cars reflected the lights on their shiny newness, and the brilliantly lit interiors with coloured moquette upholstery and white headslips looked so inviting. That was in the golden age of the steam passenger train when it reigned supreme in the world of passenger transport.

The South Island Limited

T he South Island Limited was the last new express service of the steam era; last of a long, proud lineage reaching back to the Dunedin, New Plymouth and Napier mail trains of the late 1870s. It became notable in sharing with the South Island Night Expresses the distinction of being the last steam-hauled passenger train in New Zealand. In fact, these were the last regular steam trains of any kind.

Introduced on 19 August 1949, the South Island Limiteds shed a ray of light on an otherwise dismal passenger scene, which was characterised by drastic coal shortages, shabby war-worn equipment, and dwindling passengers. The new trains represented an earnest attempt by the NZR, in spite of its problems, to stem the tide on the South Island Main Line with a faster and improved service. Plans had already been made to replace the provincial expresses with railcars. The North Island overnight expresses between Auckland and Wellington seemed assured in the meantime, and so it was logical to devote attention to the main South Island service first. Not the least of the changes was the adoption of the title of Limited, a designation which still had a magic aura attached to it in the railway world, and one which conjured up visions of the ultimate in passenger trains. The North Island had had its Limited Express between Auckland and Wellington as far back as 1924, and now the South Island was to be put on an equal footing.

The new trains, numbered 143 and 144, cut the former throughtimes of 12 hr 30 min and 12 hr 26 min to 11 hr 20 min each way. This was achieved mainly by a drastic reduction in stops from nineteen to nine, but the Limiteds were in any case the fastest 3 ft 6 in gauge trains in Australia and New Zealand. Of special benefit to Southlanders was a more convenient departure time at 8.00 a.m. in place of the traditional and rather barbaric 7.00 a.m. At the outset, Nos. 143

and 144 ran three times per week, on Monday, Wednesday and Friday, and intermediate traffic was catered for by the semi-fast Expresses Nos. 160 and 175 Christchurch-Dunedin, and Nos. 391 and 430, Dunedin-Invercargill. Nos. 145 and 174, the existing South Expresses continued to provide the service on the alternate days of Tuesday, Thursday and Saturday.

The Limited relied almost exclusively on the Hillside-built Ja engines for power. Built about the time the train was introduced, these rangy, freewheeling 4-8-2's had little difficulty in handling the demands of the tighter schedules, especially with the lighter passenger loads that eventuated. In fact, the illustrious exploits of pre-war times were overshadowed by speeds reaching into the 75 m.p.h. area, of which there are a number of reliable reports. But these speeds were to some extent facilitated by the higher track standards that had been achieved. However, against the background of speed in the air, and to a degree on modern highways, the new speeds did not have as much impact as the more modest attainments of the past. It can be said that the Limited grew up with the Ja engine, but the partnership ended with their withdrawal, and the Limited transformed into the 'Southerner', headed for the future with power partners of a far different kind in the form of the Japanese-built Dj diesel-electric locomotives.

Following the introduction of the articulated railcars and the provision of supplementary services on the main line with these vehicles, the South Island Limited was placed on a daily basis (omitting Sundays) from 13 February 1956. However, the full nineteen stops of the former Nos. 145 and 174 were reinstated. This had the effect of increasing the down and up journey times to 11 hr 55 mins and 11 hrs 50 mins, but produced faster intermediate running than ever before. A speed of 45.2 m.p.h. between Ashburton and Orari was the fastest start-to-stop in New Zealand and the 151 miles from Christchurch to Oamaru was run at 40.7 m.p.h overall. Subsequent adjustments improved the journey time further to 11 hr 40 mins in each direction. A big advantage of the daily running of the Limited was that it provided a simple, straightforward timetable for the public to follow. The complexity of the 1949 timetable had been very confusing, and to some extent had offset the benefits of the new service.

At the time of its inauguration, the normal make-up of the Limited was seven standard 56 ft cars — four seconds, seating 224 passengers, and three firsts seating 105 - plus a modern steel van to match. It was unfortunate that no new rolling stock was available and that modernisation or the provision of buffet car facilities was not undertaken, but the provision of hostesses was a welcome new service in train travel. Later the shrinking of railway passenger business had the effect of reducing the train make-up to the lowest practicable minimum of four passenger cars, but at the same time building up the rear of the train with as many as four or five Zp vans to bolster

Opposite:
Train No. 143, the South Island Limited, leaving Christchurch on a typical winter morning with the sunshine struggling to take over from the frost and fog. It is in the mid-1950s and No. 143 is powered by a Hillside Ja now standard power for the train and to remain so for the rest of its career until replaced by the diesel-hauled Southerner in 1970. The engine is readily identified as a coal-burner by the huge pile of coal in the bunker which must surely encroach upon the loading gauge. A respectable total of 8 carriages indicates that air travel and the motorcar had not yet gnawed too deeply into the South Island mainline passenger business. The time had not come when the goods vans at the rear of No. 143 could on occasion outnumber the carriages.

up the train's revenue in off-peak times.

The South Island Limited was superseded by the refurbished diesel-electric hauled 'Southerner' in December 1970 when long-awaited buffet car facilities became a reality and the overall time was substantially cut to approximately 10 hours.

The South Island Limited departing from Christchurch in the early 1960s. A silhouette of the rather formidable mass of the new Christchurch Station dominates the background. Only recently opened in November 1960, the station really had its roots in the late 1930s, in the later stages of the Great Passenger Era, and it was incongruous that when it did finally eventuate, the South Island Limited was the only daily passenger train of any consequence left to make use of the fine facilities.

The Otago Central Passenger Train

The Otago Central is a railway of precipitous and rocky gorges with associated grades, curves, tunnels, cuttings, and viaducts. There are open plains and gaunt sweeping landscapes. In fact, much of the Central is reminiscent of the famous Denver and Rio Grande Railroad. Briefly, the route follows the course of the Taieri River, first through the Taieri Gorge, then over the Strath-Taieri Plain, calling at Middlemarch, its centre, and then through the Upper Gorge almost to Waipiata. Further on, the line crosses the high Maniototo Plain and runs through Ranfurly, high above sea level, climbs over Rough Ridge, the highest point on the line, into the Ida Valley, then through the short but dramatic Poolburn Gorge into the Manuherikia Valley which leads to Alexandra. From there, the route follows the Clutha River upstream with the final thirteen miles in the Cromwell Gorge adjoining State Highway No. 8.

The Otago Central eludes any ready categorisation. Its length (146 miles from Wingatui junction), its major engineering works, and the wide territory it served, belong more to the provincial or secondary mainline. But the sparse population of the countryside, the smallness of the towns served (in 1939 Cromwell's population was 730 and Alexandra's 870), and the line's modest volume of traffic made it more akin to a branchline operation. In the public timetables the line was referred to both as the Otago Central Railway and the Otago Central Branch, with the latter more frequent. There has been the same ambiguity with passenger train services. Prior to 1900 passengers were carried on mixed trains. Passenger trains ran from 1900 until World War I when there was a reversion to mixed trains. With the exception of a summer season passenger train introduced in 1925, these remained the mainstay of passenger services until 1936 when regular daily passenger trains were re-introduced.

Overleaf:
The year is 1959, and the train is a fifteen-car Alexandra Blossom Festival special working the Taieri Gorge. This must be one of the most appealing shots ever taken through the car window, of double-heading Ab's at work, and typifies the Ab in action. The Ab was the most numerous and ubiquitous class of engine to run on the NZR.

OTAGO CENTRAL BRANCH, WITH CROMWELL-WANAKA-QUEENSTOWN MOTOR CONNECTIONS—(Week-days).

DOWN

Height ab. sea. (Ft.)	Miles	DOWN	345 am	am (Second class only)
6	..	Dunedin† to *dep*	7 52	11 45
130	9	Wingatui Jn. *arr*		..
..	..	Wingatui Jn. *dep*	8 24	12 22
492	15	Salisbury ..	•	•
401	17	Talorna ..	•	•
182	19	Parera ..	•	•
199	22	Mount Allan ..	•	
210	..	Little Mt. Allan	•	..
220	24	Christmas Creek	•	..
241	25	Hindon† ..	9 24	1 43
313	28	Deep Stream ..	•	•
623	31	Flat Stream ..	•	•
787	35	The Reefs ..	•	•
817	37	Pukerangi ..	10 3	2 47
686	41	Matarae ..	•	•
625	44	Sutton ..	•	•
663	46	Middlemarch ..	10 38	4 5
738	52	Ngapuna ..	•	•
831	56	Rock and Pillar	•	•
1089	64	Hyde ..	11 19	5 30
1107	65	Hyde Township ..	•	•
1063	69	Tiroiti ..	•	•
1120	74	Kokonga ..	11 49	6 22
1180	81	Waipiata ..	12 3	•
1302	85	Ranfurly† *arr*	‡12 15	7 15
..	..	Ranfurly *dep*	12 40	..
1767	94	Wedderburn ..	•	..
1642	101	Oturehua ..	1 18	..
1452	106	Ida Valley ..	•	..
1463	109	Auripo ..	•	..
1087	115	Lauder ..	•	..
999	120	Omakau ..	2 6	..
731	127	Chatto Creek ..	•	..
521	133	Galloway ..	•	..
490	137	Alexandra ..	2 50	..
555	143	Clyde ..	3 5	..
591	148	Doig's ..	•	..
614	152	Waenga ..	•	..
620	155	Cromwell *arr*	3 45	..

(Motor)	M, Tu, Th, Fri.		Sat.
Cromwell *dep*	4 20	4 0	6 15
Wanaka *arr*	6 0	6 0	..
Queenstown *arr* (via Arrowtown)	..	6 15	8 30

UP

(Motor)	Tu, Th, Sat. am	Tu, Th, am
Queenstown *dep* (via Arrowtown)	..	6 45
Wanaka *dep*	7 30	..
Cromwell *arr*	9 0	8 45

Miles	UP	852 Daily am
..	Cromwell to *dep*	9 10
4	Waenga ..	•
8	Doig's ..	•
13	Clyde ..	9 50
18	Alexandra ..	10 2
23	Galloway ..	•
29	Chatto Creek ..	•
36	Omakau ..	10 47
40	Lauder ..	•
47	Auripo ..	•
50	Ida Valley ..	•
54	Oturehua ..	11 37
62	Wedderburn ..	•
70	Ranfurly† *arr*	‡12 13
70	Ranfurly *dep*	12 38
75	Waipiata ..	12 49
81	Kokonga ..	1 2
86	Tiroiti ..	•
91	Hyde Township ..	•
91	Hyde ..	1 34
99	Rock and Pillar ..	•
104	Ngapuna ..	•
108	Middlemarch ..	2 15
112	Sutton ..	•
115	Matarae ..	•
119	Pukerangi ..	2 46
121	The Reefs ..	•
124	Flat Stream ..	•
128	Deep Stream ..	•
131	Hindon† ..	3 29
132	Christmas Creek ..	•
134	Little Mt. Allan ..	..
134	Mount Allan ..	•
137	Parera ..	•
139	Talorna ..	•
141	Salisbury ..	•
147	Wingatui Jn. ..	4 28
155	Dunedin† *arr*	4 54

* Stops only when required to pick up or set down passengers.   † Refreshment-room station.   ‡ Stops for lunch.

Passengers for Queenstown, Wanaka, Arrowtown, Hawea via Cromwell, may obtain through tickets at any officered station. For motor services, see page 181.

The event of the afternoon at Cromwell — the arrival of No. 345. This photo was taken in December 1939, at the end of what was by far the longest branchline in New Zealand.

These new trains (Nos 345 and 352) reduced travel time from 10 hours on the mixed trains to 7½ hours. They were made up with wooden Mainline cars of the 1920s. In 1939 two cars on each train were replaced by new steel Mainline cars with bucket seats in the first class and 'wrap around' roofs. At about this time, too, Ab engines which first appeared on the Central in 1937 shared more and more duties with the A class.

Regrettably, Nos. 345 and 352 were short-lived. Perhaps it was all too good to last. Daily running was stopped in 1945 owing to the vicious coal-saving cuts, reducing the service to three days per week. The postwar drift in passenger business did the rest, and in 1951 the trains bowed out altogether as a regular service. There was even a regression to mixes until railcars were introduced in 1956.

In retrospect we see 1936-45 as being the spring tide of passenger service on the Otago Central. The gorges, the sweeping landscapes, the swarms of rabbits in cuttings, the poplars, the lonely stations, and the daylong drumming of our A's exhaust were all memorable, but I think the crossing at Ranfurly was the highlight. It seemed to crystallise all the informality and charm of an upcountry railway operation, the unwonted bustle, the mingling of locals and passengers, the air of expectancy, and the muffled sound of No. 354's whistle coming upwind over the plain. Ranfurly must be a much less exciting place nowadays at midday.

Shortly after clearing two tunnels, the Cromwell-Dunedin passenger train crosses over the impressive steel and masonry Poolburn viaduct, 358 ft long and 121 ft high.

The West Coast Express

The main Christchurch-Greymouth-Hokitika passenger service was popularly known as the West Coast Express, or on the Coast itself simply as The Express, even though more modestly classified in the Working Timetable as the Greymouth Mail Train, and beyond Greymouth as the Hokitika Passenger southbound, and the Greymouth Mixed northbound. There would be many who would claim that the West Coast Express was the most memorable steam passenger train in New Zealand rail. Nowhere else was there such a variety and content of railway and scenic appeal as could be enjoyed from this train.

Wonderful scenery was projected through the car windows for hours on end; the incomparable magnificence of the Southern Alps, the misty forests of Westland, the sustained run along the banks of the Waimakariri, Bealey, Otira, Teramakau and Grey rivers. Always remembered is the pleasurable anticipation felt on the westbound run as No. 149 approached the mountains from across the plains, especially on a fine day when the sun shone on the snowy heights with a dazzling brilliance.

There were also the remarkable engineering works — the high viaducts and the succession of tunnels in the Waimakariri Gorge area, the lengthy wood pile bridges over the wide snow rivers, the numerous rows of high groynes protecting the river banks, all climaxed by the celebrated Otira Tunnel through the main divide.

Added to all this was a variety of operational detail to match the scenery. There were no fewer than four changes of engine in the 169 miles to Hokitika — a Christchurch engine to Arthur's Pass, electric locomotives through the tunnel, a West Coast engine to Greymouth, and another on to Hokitika. In the reverse direction, the Express started out from Hokitika as a lowly mixed

CHRISTCHURCH – GREYMOUTH MAIL TRAINS AND CONNECTIONS.

DOWN.

			Tu, Th, Sat. am		Ashburton to Darfield Junction.			Daily. am
CHRISTCHURCH	..	dep.	10 0		Ashburton	..	dep.	8 15
DARFIELD JUNCTION	..	dep.	10 52		Rolleston	..	arr.	d 9 40
SPRINGFIELD	..	arr.	11 25					Tu, Th, Sat.
SPRINGFIELD	..	dep.	11 33		Rolleston	..	dep.	9 51
					Darfield Junction	..	arr.	10 46
ARTHUR'S PASS	..	dep.	1 42		Stillwater to Reefton.			
OTIRA	..	arr.	2 4				Mon.	Not Mon.
			Dinner.				pm	pm
OTIRA	..	dep.	2 29		Stillwater	.. dep.	4 57	4 23
STILLWATER	..	arr.	e 3 57		Reefton	.. arr.	7 3	6 24
GREYMOUTH	..	arr.	4 29		Greymouth to Hokitika.			
							M. W. F.	Tu. Th. Sat.
							pm	pm
					Greymouth, dep.		4 45	4 45
					Hokitika .. arr.		6 14	6 4
					Greymouth to Westport.			
								Tu, Th, Sat.
								pm
					Greymouth (motor)	dep.		4 30
					Westport	.. arr.		7 45

UP.

			Tu, Th, Sat. am		Westport to Greymouth.			Tu, Th, Sat. am
GREYMOUTH	..	dep.	10 18		Westport (motor)	.. dep.		6 30
STILLWATER	..	dep.	10 49		Greymouth	.. arr.		9 45
OTIRA	..	arr.	12 41		Hokitika to Greymouth.			am
			Dinner.		Hokitika	.. dep.		8 30
OTIRA	..	dep.	1 6		Greymouth	.. arr.		10 5
ARTHUR'S PASS	..	dep.	1 46		Reefton to Stillwater.			
SPRINGFIELD	..	arr.	3 32				Mon.	Not Mon.
							am	am
SPRINGFIELD	..	dep.	3 38		Reefton	.. dep.	8 0	8 40
					Stillwater	.. arr.	9 57	10 39
DARFIELD JUNCTION	..	dep.	f 4 8		Darfield Junction to Ashburton.			
CHRISTCHURCH	..	arr.	5 0					Tu, Th, Sat.
								pm
					Darfield Junction	.. dep.		4 14
					Rolleston	.. arr.		g 4 56
								Daily.
					Rolleston	.. dep.		5 39
					Ashburton	.. arr.		7 6

d Change for Darfield.　　　*e* Change for Reefton.　　　*f* Change for Rolleston.　　　*g* Change for Ashburton.

For intermediate times, see pages 116, 117 (Christchurch – Greymouth – Westport); 114 (Greymouth – Hokitika); 112, 113 (Stillwater – Reefton).

Opposite:
The guard signals to the driver of Ab-806 as the engine inches back on to the West Coast Express at No. 1 Platform, Christchurch, on Tuesday 3 May 1949. There was always admiration for the precision control of the drivers on this manoeuvre; coupling-up was seldom more than a gentle nudge scarcely noticed by passengers.

Driver Jack Williams and coach foreman 'one ton' Smith check over the train advice instructions covering the run of No. 149 from Christchurch to Arthur's Pass, a routine incident of the 1940s.

which was quite a unique arrangement. And few trains have been worked by such a variety of locomotive types. On the Canterbury side, Ab's, Kb's Ja's and even G's, worked the trains, although the Ab predominated. Electric locomotives took over the tunnel section, and on the West Coast side, Q's and A's were used to Greymouth, with Wd's, Uc's and for a time Ub's working the Hokitika section of the train. Another interesting facet of operation was a piggy-back service for motorists that operated on the express between Otira and Springfield.

The Express was a West Coast institution, like the famous 'open house' hotels, whitebaiting on the Grey River, Sunday football, and seeing films in the old wooden Opera House. 'Going over on Saturday's Express', was part of the local vernacular, and if life on the Coast ever seemed restricted, the Express was the way to the wider world beyond the Southern Alps.

In addition to being the lifeline of communities on the West Coast, the express was well known to a large number of tourists as the first stage in a trip to the famous Fox and Franz Joseph glaciers. Bus services from Hokitika were usually run in conjunction with the express and left for the south the following morning.

There was almost a mythical element to the West Coast Express, in that it journeyed to the West Coast which has always been regarded as a remote and rather legendary part of New Zealand, and even after the opening of the Otira Tunnel this feeling persisted. The mountains also ensured that the train remained important and well patronised much longer than elsewhere because of the cost and difficulty of building roads through them. It was not until 1968 that a regular air service was established between the East and West coasts.

The West Coast Express endured for over thirty years — from 1924 to 1956, when it was superseded by railcars. For most of its life it ran three days per week, on Tuesdays, Thursdays and Saturdays, in each direction, with daily running over the holiday periods, but early in the war a Monday service was added as well.

The 'snow specials' were a well-known feature of this line. Right from the beginning people took advantage of the easy opportunity provided by the railway to visit the mountains. On Sunday 10 October 1926 two specials took more than 800 passengers to Otira from Christchurch and another special from Greymouth took over 600 passengers to Arthur's Pass. These were the fourth series run since July of that year, and two trains were needed on each occasion. In November, a further two trains took 1,144 passengers from Christchurch to Otira, with tickets being sold out an hour before departure. In the 1950s when snow sports soared in popularity and motorcar saturation was still a few years away, the Arthur's Pass snow specials established new records. It was common for there to be more than four trains on Sundays in the season. For

An Arthur's Pass-bound snow special makes the usual servicing and refreshment stop at Springfield in September 1938 during the alpine season. The train has an Ab engine and eleven wooden mainline cars commonly used on the longer distance excursion trains of the day. The refreshment rooms are on the extreme left. Recently the station was destroyed by fire and replaced by a contemporary structure. Ahead, the snow covered Torlesse Range beckons to the excursionists.

example on 7 August 1955 the following trains operated: Ja 1240 with 11 total, Ja 1267 with 11 total, Ja 1241 with 13 total, and Kb 967 with 15. Sad to relate, Ja 1267 failed at Rolleston on the return journey and had to be removed. A remarkable feat was then performed by Ja 1241 on Train No. 3 which took the whole *twenty-four* total (mostly steel cars with a total weight of 600 tons) from Rolleston to Christchurch, covering the twelve miles to Addington in seventeen minutes.

Many other notable specials and excursions were run over the Midland Line as well. During the Depression the fares were at the all-time bargain rates of 10 shillings return from Christchurch and 15 shillings from Dunedin. Excursions from the latter city would have been among the very rare passenger movements to make use of the south leg of the triangle at Rolleston Junction. These trains were very popular in days when few people had cars, and usually comprised a long string of wooden mainline cars hauled by two engines. They travelled overnight, reaching the West Coast on Sunday mornings, whence they proceeded to picnic places such as Lake Mahinapua or The Seven Mile. Their identity was proclaimed by coloured banners pasted on the sides of the cars.

Probably the most popular and spectacular series of excursions were those run in 1933 as a result of an outbreak of Ranfurly Shield fever. In 1932 the small West Coast Rugby Union had the temerity to challenge the powerful Canterbury Union for the shield. To everyone's astonishment the Coast nearly won, being only narrowly defeated by 5 to 3. But the Coasters felt they should have won because the final whistle was blown five minutes before time when the West Coast side was in a favourable position for scoring. From the railway angle the point was that in 1933, when the Coast again made a shield challenge, excitement was at a fever pitch. Bookings for the excursion trains to Christchurch flowed in at such a rate that four specials were finally put on to cope with the enthusiastic supporters. So many cars had to be sent from Christchurch to form these trains that there was insufficient room in the car sidings at the station to accommodate them, and some had to be stored in the coal sidings on the wharf. One special originated at Ross, another at Hokitika, and the other two from Greymouth.

The trains carried a grand total of 1,802 passengers. Cheap return fares were charged as follows: from Greymouth ten shillings, Kumara eleven shillings, Hokitika eleven shillings and eight pence, Ross twelve shillings and eight pence. It was a night of unique railway activity in Greymouth. I was living there at the time and well remember the whistles of the arriving and departing excursions throughout the night, and the general air of excitement in the town as groups of rugby supporters found their way down to the station. All this impressive train lift was operated over

Opposite:
No. 176 in the Otira River
Valley.

A remarkable overhead view of No. 176 threading its way along the precarious route through the Waimakariri Gorge between Avoca and Staircase, one of the most spectacular and famous stretches of railway line in the whole of New Zealand. Apart from portraying the ruggedness of the scenery, the photo conveys a feeling for the unerring precision of a train tracking on the rails. There is a peculiar fascination about the way No. 176 lines up to take its pre-ordained dead-centre path through the tunnel ahead. A faint feather of steam pinpoints the engine ahead. Its fire will have been banked up for the tunnels by a prudent fireman, hence little if any trace of smoke.

the mountains to timetable except for one delay caused by the inevitable yokel who opened an emergency brake valve near Otira. A railway lover understandably felt some pride in this convincing demonstration of the singular ability of the railway to move huge numbers of people cheaply, quickly, and comfortably. A disappointing footnote to this story is that the West Coast rugby side was defeated by Canterbury 23 to 14. There was never another occasion for Ranfurly Shield specials to run from Christchurch to Greymouth.

The Otira Tunnel

The 8.4 km tunnel at Otira was opened in May 1923 and was lauded as the NZR's greatest engineering work, eclipsing even the much vaunted Main Trunk viaducts and spiral. It was publicised as 'the longest tunnel in the British Empire', just beating the well known Connaught Tunnel of the Canadian Pacific Railway in the Rockies by 400 metres. It was by far the longest tunnel in New Zealand until the completion of the Rimutaka Tunnel in 1954. The circumstances of the construction of the Otira Tunnel in the heart of the Southern Alps with its associated works make it the greater engineering achievement. Besides being long, it was steep, with a falling grade of 1 in 33 from the eastern portal. Electrification was essential, and the line was wired through the tunnel and three miles beyond to Otira and fed at 1500 volts D.C. from a steam power station at Otira. English Electric Co. locomotives (class Eo) were used, with straight forward box cabs on twin four-wheeled bogies, which gave good service until replaced in 1968 by new Japanese electrics.

The exit from the eastern portal of the Otira Tunnel was a dramatic moment. You had left Westland at the other end and were now in Canterbury. 'What's the weather like?' was the question on everyone's lips. There could be dramatic variations in weather conditions on both sides of the Divide, perhaps heavy rain at Otira, changing to bright sunshine at Arthur's Pass where the westbound mail was usually waiting for the crossing where electric units were changed over. Here 'happy' Anderson, the train magazine and sweets vendor, a well-known character of the trains in the 1930s also changed over. 'Happy' was a short rotund gentleman with a pink face and a curved stem pipe which he puffed contentedly whenever he had the chance. His pile of reading matter included the *Grey River Argus*, *The Women's Journal*, *Humour* and those splendid English magazines of the time, *The Strand* and *The Wide World*. He was the concessionaire of the Greymouth Railway Station bookstall for many years, this being looked after by his equally cheerful daughter Sybil while he was away on the trains.

In those days all the main passenger trains were served by these travelling vendors. There were other well-remembered railway personalities of West Coast trains: guards like dapper Bert O'Neill with his waxed moustache, immaculate uniform and cap set at a rakish angle, greeting passengers as he worked his way through the train with his big lantern under his arm. There was amiable gangling, ginger-headed Bob Gilmour, and Percy Callan who, legend had it, operated a cobblers shop in the guard's van of 'The Perishable' during its nocturnal rambles. People like these combined with the trains themselves to make NZR the great public institution it had become.

Uc-362 arriving at Greymouth with the Hokitika-Christchurch Express service on Tuesday 9 May 1950. A-423 waits in the loop with the extra cars put on the train at Greymouth.

New Zealand rail was a social institution as well as a great national carrier of passengers and freight. At no time was this involvement deeper than during wartime. Railway stations were associated with some of wartime's most emotional moments — the sad farewells as crowded troop trains drew away from crowded platforms, and the joyous receptions when the trains brought the soldiers home again for a heroes' welcome.

The railways played an indispensable role in both World Wars, wearing out trains, tracks and men in the process. Passenger traffic reached astronomical dimensions; during World War II ordinary passengers rose from a pre-war average of eight million to an all-time record of eighteen million in the year ended 31 March 1944. The upper photo shows a troop train ready to leave for Burnham with Westland Volunteers in October 1939. The lower photo, taken in April 1940, shows Second Echelon troops crowding another eastbound troop special.

The scene at Cora Lynn on Thursday 12 May 1949 at 3 p.m. as Ab-610 at the head of the Greymouth-Christchurch Express quietly simmers while waiting for Kb-970 on a load of westbound empties to enter the loop. The beefy silhouette of the Kb with its implications of vast power is unmistakable. It may sound like heresy in some quarters, but there always seemed to be an incongruity between the huge size of the Kb and the comparatively Lilliputian dimensions of the four-wheeler wagons they hauled, especially when the latter were empty. The Kb engine made much more sense (aesthetically) at the head of a long train of the much larger passenger vehicles.

A returning passenger special from Arthur's Pass to Christchurch approaches the Waimakariri Crossing from the west side somewhere around 1920. Two dainty Baldwin Ub tenwheelers are supplying the power up front, and judging by the make-up of the train it could have been some kind of Ministerial Special. The first car is a Ministerial car, the second a diner, the third and fourth are new mainline cars, the fifth a 'birdcage', and the sixth an American saloon car. Quite a sampler of NZR coaching stock of the period. A curious feature is a single L-wagon sandwiched behind the engine.

Acknowledgements

Apart from photographs from J.D. Mahoney's own collection of photographs, the author would like to acknowledge the following photographic sources:

Alexander Turnbull Library, 92, 146
Auckland Public Library, 6, 22, 59, 88, 107, 139, 145
A.C. Bellamy, 91, 110
H. Bennett, 144, 146
J.D. Buckley, 57
Canterbury Museum, 115
J.A. Dangerfield, 94, 97
Dominion Museum, 87
Hardwicke Knight Collection, 120
Levin Weekly News, 74
R.J. Meyer, 54
NZ Herald, 28, 47, 76, 107, 111, 141
NZ Railway & Locomotive Society, 32, 73
NZ Railways Publicity, 24, 27, 43, 49, 50, 74, 80, 99, 100
W.W. Pryce, 31
A.R. Schmidt, 66, 70, 78
W.W. Stewart, 44
R.H. Stott, 96.